Freeflow Books
Copyright ©2014
ISBN: 978-1505359534
Library of Congress Catalog Card Number: Not interested.
Many paintings printed in this book are available for barter, gold and silver coin. I would trade the book for your promise to spend the rest of this life pressing on for personal liberty, doing the little and large chores of life by the dictates of your conscience. No need to advertise it. Just believe. You see, it might be best to keep low and quiet about it. The herd is a nasty thing on any hill.

Just a head nod with your best knowing look will do. And the book is yours.

Cover design by Rose Throop

The Art Crazy Old Man Knows I Am A Phony But Tells Me To Keep Painting Anyway 2014. Acrylic on canvas 36 X 48"

Art is Work

Actually, in this case, painting is work. I have never considered myself to be an artist, really. I don't even like "art", the way
my art-lover friend Dan does, one to leap at the chance to visit a
gallery or a museum. I love painting though, any kind, and at an
art show, I will make a bee line past all other forms of expression
to see work of painters, more to learn and compare than to enjoy.
Some times professional jealousy creeps in, especially when I see
rendering that has a special hair shirt quality, when each stroke of
the brush belies both a practical and encyclopedic knowledge of
control or constipation—hard to tell which for sure until I meet
the painter for beer and oysters. Unfortunately so many masters
are either dead or practically inaccessible, and from my viewpoint
in Oswego at least, painting is tolerated as a form of yoga, just
another hobby distraction to the despair of the modern age. Thank
God for family and friendship, and the blessings of the narcissist
Internet. Otherwise by now I'd be eating my toenails at a local
mental health spa.

In Providence Rhode Island I looked at my first van Gogh
through a painter's eyes. It was a religious experience. The great
and powerful Vincent was a failure. Hurray! Another human
being. It was a 14 x 17" landscape entitled *View of Auvers-sur-Oise*,
a day's work in a village north of Paris in the year he took his life. I
read into that painting like any tome of art writing could instruct.
The great Vincent van Gogh was nothing much really. Just another
proud working man, driven day after day, year after year with an
obsession to perfect his limitations. I saw the human hand laying
it on thick, always at the right place at the wrong time, a failure
at night, hopeful idiot by morning. One life to live, and if he was
determined to be a painter, to Hell with the greatest of art critics,
Mssrs. Degradation and Poverty.

It worked! A few hours coloring a French village from a field,
and he succeeded to live another day pretending to be a painter. It
was the billionaires who got rich though. They took the dignity of
pride in pretend and made a killing for themselves. Endowments
all over the world buy up van Gogh's paintings to prove unwittingly their dislocation to humanity. They "get" the history, but fear

the present moment like a pathogen. I could count all the struggling van Gogh's living today. But it would take a lifetime and
more assistants in my employ than those pretending to be artists
at a Jeff Koons factory.

One more point before my plea:

Kurt Vonnegut: "We are what we pretend to be, so we must be
careful about what we pretend to be".

Last month I checked out from the library a photo book about
Picasso. Pictures taken of him at leisure and work in 1956. A mess
of canvases and sculptures in every room, painting on the walls,
dripped paint on the floor. His mansion had twenty foot ceilings
and huge doors at the end of one studio opening out onto a balco-
ny of palm trees. "La Californie" was the name of his hermitage in
Southern France.

There is a brief passage in the book referencing his time in Mont-
martre, when he lived in poverty, painting. Somehow still able
to acquire materials without the financial support of credit cards
and/or a well-endowed sugar mama. I think poverty in 1905 was a
world of difference from what we call it today. He must have made
modern starving artists look like rich dandys sacrificing a week
of television and a bowl of chocolates for art. Or, God forbid, cell
phone service! The photos of him as a rich millionaire painting
in a mansion, juxtaposed with my imagination of a poor Parisian
painter holed up in some cold January flat over a hundred years
ago, instruct and educate like nobody's business. His wealthy
genius in 1956 appears unchanged over 50 years time. He looks
just as poor to me, but rich in determination and singleness of
purpose. He eats, sleeps, voids excrement, laughs and paints. There
is no stopping him. The art crazy old man.

I mention Picasso's sameness to my wife the other morning over
coffee. I asked her how differently would we live if suddenly Jeff
Koons got cast inside one of his poodles, and Ron Throop went
viral throughout the acquisition dreams of bored billionaires.
"Our coffee and climate would get better. Other than that," she
admitted, "nothing".

A few months ago I helped hang a show at our local art association. One of the helpers, a member my age, asked me what I do
for a living. "Paint," I said. "I am a painter". It was more difficult
for me to get that truism past my lips than if I told him I was an

untouchable scouring latrines with my socks.

Picasso's Picasso. Throop is Throop. We have nothing in common, besides a heightened desire to perfect our limitations. My path for the rest of this life is to pretend like Picasso. It won't hurt anybody. It won't even help. Maybe, if I just work harder and dream longer, Rose will taste a better sip of coffee with her next husband, from the Florida room of her beach condo in Boca Raton.

Now finally, an explanation.

I found out last winter that I am a Stuckist, more or less. Their manifesto is available here at the show. Take a look. The strongest statement, #4, *Artists who don't paint aren't artists*, if not cryptic, is flat out silly wrong. I know nothing about ceramics, but I know a man, a teaching artist who would take his class to Chimney Bluffs along Lake Ontario to gather clay to be used for glazing. Ho boy! Show me a Stuckist in London who longs to extract cadmium from zinc ore. Or, take my friend the marble sculptor, who travels out of state to steal marble from parking lots. He approaches his stone like I do any canvas. As an ignoramus. I wish I had the knowledge (and time) to make my own paint and weave my own canvas. I'd rather paint on a log with berry juice, but the berry juice will never put out like my sweetheart dioxizine purple. And dioxizine sounds like painful chemical death to workers in that industry. So I just hold my breath while I paint.

Anyway, Stuckism. Good medicine. We are painter-workers. We get up in the morning to paint. We are international brothers and sisters in pretend. Yet we all need to get paid. Here is how I dream to be paid. Milton Glaser has the phrase "Art is Work" painted on the transom of his company door. Another tome of knowledge garnered from just three precious words. Art is work. The big painting I finished this week took exactly 40 hours—from surface, image, and finally to frame. At $13 dollars an hour (what I was making at my last job as "cook in the great north woods", plus materials, and "element-X" fee (30%), I value it at $832.00.

So, any takers? I'll have to add $100.00 for shipping.

There you have it! The first Oswego Stuckist to admit the truth. Art is work. So is toenail chewing if one can pretend really hard. I promise to play this game out to the end. My dreams tell me that buying up my work now, will secure some legacy to leave your children. Buy a signed book. Put it in the attic. Buy a painting to hang in the parlor. Its story will not die.

I apologize about the lack of framing for many of these paintings. The truth is I have another show going on at the Dyer Arts Center at R.I.T. in Rochester. Unlike Zink, I would be banished from furthering that avenue of pretend if I didn't deliver framed work. We're out of money now, and I blame myself for scheduling two shows in the same month. The gallerists at the Rochester venue must keep up appearances. R.I.T. needs to pretend too. And I need to pretend that I have a chance to break into a world that will provide me a line cook's salary to paint. Please, if you find my art not practical enough for your tastes, patronize Zink Shirts® in any way you can. Glenn has offered this space to local color. Come here for holiday shopping. His work is sublime and corporate killing at the same time. Wear one of his shirts and flip a tall bird at the bottom-line world of men who care not a bean about your day to day. Glenn and I do. Look, we invited you all here. Open your wallets and pick out a record album to play. But first, open your wallets!

If I Was Mao, I'd Want My Duck Hunters To Shoot Satellites Out Of Space 2014. Acrylic on canvas 18 X 24"

The Joy Of Man's Desiring Triptych 2014. Acrylic on hard board, (3) 11 X 14"

The Joy of Art Kind Of Not Really

I painted three characters from a favorite novel of mine by Jean Giono, *The Joy of Man's Desiring*. I haven't read it in some time, but I think on it often. Jourdan and Marthe are a childless old couple existing on Grémone Plateau with day to day drudgery and barely tepid emotional disturbance toward either direction on the happiness meter. Then one night Jourdan gets the urge to plow his field beneath starry skies. A saunterer approaches from the south. "The sky looks like Queen Anne's Lace," he says to Jourdan. They share a pipe and joy begins. Marthe catches on early in the novel and with Bobi's goad, takes a sack of the surplus grain and feeds it to the birds, who like Bobi, come out of nowhere to visit a place nobody ever wants to visit. Despair.

A mystery novel without a whodunit. A novel of mystery. Worth reading if you can execute your Kindle one morning and go lay down in a field with a real book and the deer ticks.

Last night I went to a couple art shows and fell asleep. The business of art. Without music. Without unchoreographed dance. Like drinking hot beer on a hot day when you're not even thirsty. One was a BFA exhibition at the college. The other a printmaking show at Zink Shirts. My wife and I went to both, and afterwards I sat in the driveway ranting for five minutes on the sorrows of a culture that is so morbidly dead, it cannot even make the joy of art manifest to desirous and wanting people.

We don't know how to live. Careful steps. A quiet view, and then on to the next "someone else's inspiration". Nobody says a thing about it. Shhh. The graduates are learning early on how to spill the soul to wipe it up quickly before it stains the carpet. Inspired work at both shows no doubt. That is how art flows through and is presented by the art-maker. But inspiration and gladness stops there, before the canvas is dry. The young people had a better crowd, more smiling faces, doting grandmothers, encouragement, awards and catering. They'll want to make art professionally, but more likely search for a creative paid position in life, and never ever make a leap or a peep at a juried art exhibition, or when stepping into a gallery, or swan diving off a tall building. Only in the 21st century can art become something this depressing.

My friend Dan is unwittingly beating with a stick the cultural

tendency to kill art with decorum. One-track minded, he will succeed. He goes to Manhattan, an Oswego bear with primal humanity, to teach a wild lesson to these uptight, unartful, millionaire
gallery dandys. Another friend, Eric, spent his Friday afternoon
grinding a stone into some shape a wine-soaked Mt. Olympus dec-
orator might purchase for Zeus' parlor. Two remembrances from
the BFA show made my driveway rant less devastating, leaving the
door a crack open for hope, more or less.

The gallery director Mike, also my friend, told the story of a job
interview he had once at a pet cemetery. If hired he would become
official headstone painter. A likeness of a cat to represent the dead
cat. A bunny, a bunny. Or just paint it the favorite color of the deceased. The 90-year-old owner was the last to interview. Mike was
told to yell into the old man's practically deaf ear. Even though it
brought my shy friend pain to do it, he did it, but not loud enough
he guessed. He wasn't hired. That story was rock n' roll. It was life.
I laughed. For me it brought meaning to all the pretty pictures
hanging on the walls.

On a wall outside the gallery was a black and white poster photo
taken in 1970 of the art faculty at the time. Some were dressed
haphazardly into costume, because artists are allowed to do that
for a group photo. One of my wife's old professors, who was in the
picture, walked me through it naming names, and pointed to his
wife in the top row. I laughed and laughed. Then he brought our
thirteen year old daughter over to the drawing teacher to get his
criticism of the sketch book always attached to her hip at these
functions. Haunting photo. Replete with twelve conflicting emo-
tions if you're foolish enough to let them mingle.

I am. Ta-da!

The reason I fall into despair from time to time is because I
am the art fool who remains a league or two behind joy, but can
easily see it and hope to get it for myself and others. Art is rock
and roll, or jazz, hip-hop, what have you. An art show is a dead
thing for most. Why? Because it is unshared. All the Bobis are out
trying their best to reanimate the clay of their sisters and brothers.
Impossible without a pow-wow, games, flash dancing, and overall
wildness. It could happen, but not with pretty pictures. The Beats
did it with wine jugs and bad poetry. Bobi succeeded with flowers,
juggling and oats to a few eager peasants of Grémone Plateau. The

painter as artist succeeds for himself only, from time to time. It is never good enough for everyone, not even anybody on the best day.

The Me culture continues to make art for the mees. Me too. But I am joining Dan on his next teaching lesson in Manhattan. I will follow through with my three-chord club idea, so I can get together with other bad guitar players and a jug of homemade wine. I'll continue to show my paintings also, but only with the caveat that the room plays the music loud.

Part II

I think Bobi is the better psyche of every man who isn't starving to death. He brought joy, hope and juggling to the oat and lentil peasants of Grémone Plateau when they needed a way out of their miserable routine. I have come back to this book in some manner every spring for the past twenty years.

I think my work can be interpreted as reactions from a man like Bobi if he was magically whisked off the plateau and set into modern times a hundred years into the future. He had the strength and sense of the best farmers among men. He could shear a sheep and create a gelding, even on a full stomach of bread and cheese. But he treasured most the fool in the man who can make the hardest of lives livable with minimal, but repeated effort of color and comedy. Make flowers grow out the kitchen window where the cash crop was sown. Use the grain surplus to feed starving songbirds, so songs can be heard. Flowers and song and a pipe to smoke. Then off in the night to save the next sodden clump of dirt farmers plagued with the worry of how life should go.

Poor Bobi. Poor us. He materialized in the brown salt grass beside the highway in March, took a thoughtful look around, spied the dead deer unnamed and untouched sunk in the fine gravel, and promptly leapt on to the road to meet the grill of a speeding Mack truck.

Part III

Dan dropped off some paint and a couple canvases to my surprise and wonder. Then, he came back the next day with more paint and canvases. He also rolled up several Arts sections of the New York Times so Rose and I could be entertained with human good news over our morning coffee. I am a ditch digger of wealth and taste.

There was an article about Milton Glaser collaborating with the writer of the TV show *Madmen*. In it the reporter referenced the door of Glaser's company bearing the words, "Art is Work" on the transom glass.

Yes! That is what this famous graphic artist is worth to me. Passing on a truism that I will take to the grave. Art is work. One, two, perhaps a cliff drop in salary grade from ditch digger. However, even with all the maneuvering to paint in awkward positions, I will never wake with a slipped disk and a painful drive to the next work site. So in matters of health and possible longevity, I save big time by being a painter. I work. I just don't work for a living… Yet. Rose is making an investment in my education. She is putting me through life art school. She works. I cook the rice and beans. We eat together. She grabs my hand and admonishes me for the dirt under my fingernails. The paint dirt!

And what do I have to show for it?

A small house filled up with much more than a repeated yarn or two expressed at the shuffleboard court about that awesome French drain I dug back in the summer of '98.

Unart Town

Our town is so devoid of art venues. I need to display my music player at a show in June. There is a screen printing shop in operation by the river in the process of convincing me that there are no other galleries worth art's time. The proprietor offered the space to me. I am over-obliged, and here is why.

It is a huge space, dark, maybe dank, but full of life, youthful, unpretentious, and dreamy like rock n' roll at seventeen. The owner, Glenn, has the right idea. He prints shirts and stuff, and offers musicians and artists a gathering place. In five years he will be able to boast saving egos, marriages and perhaps even a life or two. In the last two days he has hosted pro bono art on the level it must be raised to, if humanity is to carry on for another thousand years. On Friday there was a performance art gig organized by my friend, the college gallerist and his buddy, the sculpture professor. Last night, a benefit for another teacher-artist who had a heart attack a couple months ago, but as adjunct, was uninsured. Last month another artist friend, and also a teacher, set up a sumi ink station on the floor during open mike. My wife and I had a date with our daughter. We got to be ageless and stroke newsprint paper with fat bristle brushes.

Zink Shirts® is the Island of Misfit Toys, and Oswego artists, Santa's not-forgotten poor girls and boys. Small town middle-aged men and women mingling with inspired youth not yet crushed by the weight of vanity; themselves ready to become misfits, but most will lack the courage to remain, and move to the big city and struggle to make art for the artless. I plan to teach them at Zink not to bother—to just "get a job and some place to live". To make art their living, whenever possible. If a big break comes, take it, but give back to Zink Shirts®. Every town should have a meeting place to feel. The counting houses posing as bars, restaurants, and hip and hop retail have played host to the twaddle of finance for too long. They don't want to know anything about you past your purse. It works for them, and the people suffer for it. To me American towns appear twisted like the gangrened insides of a moaning zombie, rather than the healthy paradise such incredible wealth could reveal. Walk up the main street of my town on a late April

Music Box 2010. Acrylic on birch 22 X 24 X 38"

afternoon. Pottersville.

I am a 47 year old father and house-husband who paints. I have been applying my vanity to the undeserving New York "art" scene for several years now. To hell with the gallery wizards and witches. Their coven on Manahatta brews soulless international bunk to don the palaces of millionaire twits. The business of art. Ha! I call it the undertaker of happiness medicine. My healing place is wherever I feel ageless at the moment. For dinner, the culinary arts. For family, time without appointment. For freedom, my art to pull me back to love. For society, a place like Zink Shirts®, where I can stand proud, a fellow failure in solidarity. Glenn has a loading dock, and behind the dock the bands play in "The Dark Room". On Friday night I played dead there on stage while my friend laid a quilt and dried sticks over me. A flautist played and he joined in with an Irish round drum. I was able to keep still for the performance even though I got a charley horse in my shoulder.

Flashback to 1983 under the trestle with my best friends. Boone's Farm Strawberry Hill, an eight-pack of Matt's Beer, and the girl on Cypress Avenue. Another night of performance art at Zink Shirts®.

How Just One Week Can Silence a Tree

Thoreau wrote, "Public opinion is a weak tyrant compared with our own private opinion. What a man thinks of himself, that it is which determines, or rather indicates, his fate".

To take his meaning to heart, I must be in a roller-coaster relationship with myself. Yet then I get wise eventually and consider the source. Thoreau had no one to love or be loved with, no children to raise, no mornings to wake up in slight terror of the dependency of his growth on another. Mrs. Emerson would give him a cold turkey leg if he cleaned out the chicken coop whether or not he waved a fist at the sky that morning. No other human being really cared about his emotional fluctuations, unless they instigated new behavior from the ax he carried into the woods. Thoreau was a bachelor whom nobody needed. So he was only a philosopher in part. One can't think out people problems if one is not among the people. Can't be a father or a mother if he was never a parent. And remember, Buddha, who was a father, abandoned his wife and child to befriend someone else's buffalo boy. That living might deliver a kind of lizard wisdom, but no human philosophy worth sharing among my kind.

So the financially unsuccessful painter's life wreaks havoc sometimes in the mind of the man who irrationally clings to traditional roles handed down from generation to generation. What's new in this modern world? Me and the family eat and sleep, one of us found a job and a place to live. I know how to cook, paint with acrylics, write, fold laundry, sift cat litter, care for parakeets, a wife and children. I am not the tree in the paintings. Metaphorically, I am more like the weather, and the tree represents those affected by me. It tolerates my presence for both the good and bad I bring today. Stay temperate over long stretches of time, though, or lose their trust. No hurricanes. No tornadoes. No blow-downs. But no southern California either. For Pete's sake, you're an artist, not an accountant.

Same Tree A Week Apart 2012. (2) Acrylic on hard board 14 X 18"

Our School Board Voted To Keep Childhood Concussion and Can The Alternative School

In America, school districts rather have non-thinking kids jar their yogurt brains than push for academic excellence. In art as in life, critical thinking has been removed from education. Students are taught art by experts educated in colleges and universities. As if Diego Rivera ever had even a toothbrush in common with a Jeff Koons. The bankers, politicians, corporatists with their small army of propagandists, all educated by avarice, repeat "art is what the media says it is".

This painting will show at my local art association. It is a visual classroom, debate club, cultural criticism. Perhaps 50 people will see it and be moved by it in some way other than a multi-million dollar Gagosian wet dream. Wheel in the Koons poodle and maybe a rich old lady will buy it because it reminds her of her own dear deceased dog, the only living soul she ever loved.

My painting is neither good nor bad art. It is life in America that everyone understands and certainly can react to. The poor Whitney cannot discern what's going on in its own country. A Koons retrospective! Millionaires and billionaires jonesing for another catered party of the elite. Harvard educated in the arts is oxymoronic like Wall Street prepped in divinity. Yet they both get along very well at the same dumbed-down parties.

Art needs content. Faith has faded. Antibiotics and Mick Jagger have really done our psyches a bad turn.

Without a judgmental king or capricious God, modern, wealthy societies have no fear marker to guide them. No indelible code of conduct. Today our children are abandoned to the concept of making it up as they go. Acceptance of societal degeneration is the parental new black. And of course if the rabbi, minister, tribal chief, or imam are not controlling the media, then we get more live and let live lost souls reporting on what is right and wrong. Doomed to failure. Exponential failure with few ideas for change.

I have one.

Diego Rivera art back into the mainstream. Use art to teach. Do not teach about art. Stop retelling the lives of the lucky few. They suck our nation's creativity dry and confuse the hell out of everyone.

Our School Board Voted To Keep Childhood Concussion And Can The Alternative School 2014. Acrylic on canvas 32 X 24"

School Board Letter Rough Draft

I attended my first school board meeting last week. This year our daughter has entered school (7th grade) and I was curious how a superintendent thousandaire would manage a 78 million dollar budget for a town of about 19,000. He had five big screen flatscreens set up in the cafeteria to present his Powerpoint. Cuts. Always cuts. Slashings and mashings. Money. Always money gained by austerity. 2 million. $762,540.00. Custodial positions, theater manager, technicians, one teacher from each discipline, the alternative education school, all standing in line at the chopping block. They wait patiently for a small time hack accountant to determine their fate, which never arrives with a positive back-slapping these days— never a "great job Mr. or Ms. Math," or "Fine work Charlie Tech," now the kids are ready to play adult in the new age. Thank you for your service. You are number one".

No. More like, "Your job is tenuous at best. You are lucky to have it. Me and this board of dumb yokels whom I can lead blind (mostly because of my suit and paycheck) dangle your job security always a day out of reach. We don't give a damn about your credentials nor dedication. By law you can't even strike. Ha-ha. By golly, even a ditch digger can strike!"

Mr. Superintendent wants to fire them all. He is the new guy with the big ideas. His initiative for the 2013-14 school year was a goal for improved attendance. Each kid with perfect attendance would get a desktop printed certificate at the end of the year. Little Johnny can have pneumonia, but come to school anyway to cough a hardy virus all over the classroom. When the superintendent gets a head cold, he stays home to watch rerun episodes of *Breaking Bad*. He has sick days and personal days and vacation days written in to his contract. Tater tots and USDA slightly approved ground beef for the little scholars to assuage the hunger pangs and hold each struggling immune system at the "my eyes are open sometimes, so I must be alive" level.

Big ideas. Here is one.

Fire administration. Obtain retired accountants and financial planners pro bono with the caveat that the new budget scraps everything besides teachers, materials, janitors, cafeteria workers and bus drivers. Keep the classes diverse and interesting. For lunch, serve a fresh green salad, brown rice, slice of cheddar cheese and an apple, and have buses stop only at designated pick up points.

There is so much to write about on this subject. I must end my primer for the day. I see a book building.

I shall leave readers with two anecdotes to strengthen the argument for school board tar and feathering.

My father's school district has fired the last two superintendents. However, the contract for each was a guaranteed five-year pay plan, even if the job was terminated. The first was let go after one year. The second made it for two years and was fired. At present, both are getting full pay from the district while the third considers his options. And the tater tots are still constipating the kids.

My friend the music teacher worked in a district south of Utica. The superintendent there resigned over threat of sexual harassment charges brought against him. My school board in Oswego soon hired him to principal one of its elementary schools.

He hit on the teachers there.

And resigned after several complained.

Now he is the superintendent of schools in Lake Placid, N.Y.

Insulation. Don't tell anyone. The education mafia. My locals, my yokels. All of them high on their private cheeseburger power trips.

School Board Final Draft

Dear Superintendent and members of the board,

I write with an opinion on the April 8th public address in the high school cafeteria. Nice turnout. People get upset when their jobs go south. I get upset when education becomes an accountant's pet project.

Our seventh grader summed up my thoughts best this morning over her waffle. "So the proposal is to fire security, custodians, theater manager and technician and teachers across the board, including all of mine at the Buc, and this will benefit my education? Seems like the superintendent has his priorities backwards".

Wider class ratios in a less clean and less safe school district?

A nearly 80 million dollar budget, and there are no cuts to be made that will keep the jobs already in place. Really?

Oswego needs new ideas. A fresh outlook. Maybe even an old one dug up from the past. Look at a yearbook from 1960. Count up every paid position, match it to the budget of the time, and research why it has come to be that multiple millions of dollars cannot support a thriving student body in small town New York. Why does it always come down to a need of more money?

Oh yes, the mandates. Pensions, rising salaries, common core, insurance! Yes, of course. Like we're all going to jail if we don't abide by the corrupt political directives from Albany and Washington. What? The excuses are so many. But it boils down to this. The superintendent and the school board should not be in such a determinate position of financial power. Not one board member is properly trained, either ethically, morally, or economically to deal with this level of responsibility.

These are our children and this is our money. We need to set up a new structure to distribute the tax levy squarely and fairly. Perhaps more democracy, maybe less. This coming to the table every couple of years to manipulate the community investment is an abject failure. Fresh ideas abound, all of them are linked to a new philosophy.

Eliminate the Buc school because this year's money-manager says the board made a boo-boo two years ago? Hire professional educators just to fire them when the whim hits the new guy with the 100,000 + salary? Which of you deserves that incredible power? We didn't give it to you willingly. We got a crooked paradigm passed down to us. Vote every couple years from a shallow pool of the politically/economically correct to eventually be steamrolled by the corporate or political heads of the system—themselves well pensioned and insulated by their own political power. The education mafia.

Certainly there are retired accountants, bankers, financial planners residing in the county who would agree to work alongside retired educators to plan and execute budgets pro bono? The superintendent could have listed his own job to be considered for the chopping block. What is his contract worth the district? His pension? If the state mandates the position of superintendent, what does the board think will happen to Oswego schools if it votes to ignore any bogus mandate the state decrees? Will Albany send the troopers in to close down the schools?

A change in philosophy.

Retired teachers, grandmothers and grandfathers, could they not be easily trained to teach at the elementary levels, through volunteering?

Why ax the theater and not sports?

Eliminate the athletic budget entirely. Allow only those games the gym teachers can oversee during class time. Red Creek doesn't have a football team. Should it? Will they fire another teacher so a niche group of kids can seek their first concussion? An education is not a football team. However, a theater is by nature interdisciplinary. Also, all of us are inspired every day by theater training. Who hasn't watched television, or viewed a movie or a play in his or her lifetime? Our school is not a football team. Nor, for that matter, should it be a nationwide traveling marching band.

Take my advice. Study history in order to learn from it. Are any of you on the board happy with the way things are in the community? Any opinion on the new style of underwear exposed bow-legged walking of our young men? The meth labs popping up all over the city? I go to get a haircut for Thanksgiving dinner, and it's like I walked into a maximum security prison conversation. Turn on the radio to hear what the kids are listening to. The little kids. It's Nicki Minaj, and she's gyrating good news about teenage pregnancy. Is it any different from the Everly Brothers pleading for Suzy to wake up? Yes it is. A world of difference. The English teacher who taught my Dad and Mom, was there twenty years later to teach my sister and me. A position was made and it was guaranteed, and he lived to teach a proud career.

Here in Oswego we are building a reputation where the board hires teachers to fire them on a financial whim. And the superintendent retires with an annual salary four times the Oswego family average.

Why stay in school to participate in a bleak future? Unlike 1960 there is no industry in upstate New York. No one starts at the bottom hoping to work his way up anymore. A high school education is no guarantee for a better life anywhere. For so many in Oswego, the bottom is already at the top. The superintendent inspired cuts are just bringing us down further and showing our kids a new low.

My suggestions to the board:

Study history and economics to research why such huge sums cannot educate our children properly.

Eliminate all sports and band that involve travel.

Hire a volunteer superintendent as a respected, unpaid position for the community.

Agree in writing never to cut a position once it is instituted unless population decrease justifies the cut.

Thank you for your time.

Ronald Throop

P.S.

I shall not come to a meeting again until you change the structure of it. Not allowing names to be named, only positions, was not only absurd, but also arrogant beyond comfort. A kind of adult bully-ism. These are our children and grandchildren, and all of yours too. We know the teachers by name. So do you. The board sanctions disrespect with this "meeting" procedural. It is embarrassing to watch. Teachers are professionals with respectable careers. Treat them accordingly.

My Six-fingered Hand Is Dry Like A California Pancake 2014.
Acrylic on canvas 16 X 20"

Anti-Gun

I am phallically anti-gun in spring. Both right and left wing vitriol are like burning whiskey shots in a country bar full of twenty-thirty something male drunks and a handsome couple at the end of the bar, stopped in to call a mechanic who'll come tow their car broke down up the road. They are on a romantic getaway to California and dreading the immediate future of this present moment setback.

The local drunks get talkative. The cue ball cracks louder. Half the men start eying the wife, and all of them snarl their best profundities, which might involve an ATV clash with a tree, last week's drunken brawl, or a threat to another and another's ugly mother. Louder and angrier. More whiskey. A boilermaker. And then, God help the hapless traveling couple, *political opinions*. Each drunk dude will have five, and all five will be the same five as the talking heads had on the radio shows during the week. Whether it was Diane Rehm or Rush Limbaugh, official opinions have been successfully injected—now to disseminate them throughout monkey land, and observe similar simian opinions no matter how remote and degenerate the watering hole.

The couple gets wise. They know that the following Saturday night shall bring the next round of official opinions from state media. Kids will shoot kids. Drones will bomb kids. And adults will drink to oblivion defending a culture that went sputnik the day after the last shadow was counted on a Hiroshima rock. Bonnie grabs hold of the machine gun under her coat; Clyde grabs the only set of keys within reach and pulls the pin on his hand grenade. Out the door, ba-BOOM! Rat-a-tat-tat-tat, and a race down lover's lane to California in some Chevy built tough truck with two balls dangling from the trailer hitch.

Moral of the story: "Might is right", or, "Opinions are a weak puppy to the belief with the rolled up newspaper", or finally, "Freedom is free to romantic couples well-armed and anonymous, but only for a limited time".

Back Of Rose 20 Years Ago 2014.
Acrylic on canvas 11 X 14"

Rose Carries Her Books To School, Leaves Swirling

Last night we met Dan out at a screen printing warehouse that regularly hosts local talent—musicians, painters, photographers. He set up a sumi ink station by the cold wind draft garage doors and my family went to work on the large newsprint paper provided. Like the ink wash masters of pre-indoor plumbing Japan we went at it without hesitation. Unlike the masters, we didn't care if the royals liked it or not. We weren't making swirling leaf poetry. We were local yokels, imbued with our own luscious funk, out grooving with live music on a Saturday night.

However, earlier in the day, like the master's admiring gardener with some talent, I was caught in my own flux of swirling leaf poetry. I found a college photograph of Rose in the basement box and brought it to the studio window to set my morning thoughts right for paint.

A haunting photo of private beauty, lust, want, daring, and desire. From a time a year or two before we met. I painted her in front of me walking to class. I didn't know her, and she wouldn't want me. I was carrying my Whitman down to the lake. I would wash my arms and face leaning over the shore rocks of blue Ontario. I would read and journal and dream. I had a Whitman hat and soft eyes and rolled a Drum tobacco cigarette to smoke in honor of the girl I saw walking to class, the poor girl I would meet one day and marry.

Great date last night. Pow!

More Dan

Three days ago I was in A.C. Moore holding on tight to my 40% off coupon before the rows of studio canvases. Coveting. Coveting. I came very close to buying a 10-pack of 11 X 14's. I have frames for that size a friend donated last year. I could spend just a little to keep me satisfied for a week or two.

No. Must hold out. Must turn around and leave. Will power. I made a pact with my wife back in December. No art supplies purchased until our daughter gets her dowry. We will make austerity pay. Paint on the roadside curb. Paint dead leaves. Paint rocks. Just no more investment until wedding bells ring.

I made it out of the store without a purchase. Not even a $.50 squeeze bottle of tropical blue craft paint, a color I can't mix to, no matter how hard I try.

Success! Then depression, and emptying an old school desk full of nails and what-nots in the basement and bringing it up to the dining room. "Well, I guess I'll just start painting the furniture."

Paint supply depleting. Mixing with gesso. Low as a painter goes, and then...

My good friend Dan the professor stopping by last night to drop off leftover student paint and two painted canvases.

Yes, 11 X 14".

Henry Miller wrote about the magic that happened to him in a super economy whenever his need molecules began choking the ether above and below. *Big Sur and the Oranges of Hieronymus Bosch*. It's a great read for poor painters. Unfortunately, very few writers like Henry exist in the Internet age.

Thank you Dan for the creative boost. May you get to Big Sur one day. We will visit, bearing gifts of good olive oil and a bag of fresh parsley to season your humble stew.

I Show off My Incontinence Because I Love You (Image on following page)

Two lizards in love. Sometimes the one on the right expresses his joy too noisily and embarrasses his lover who goes blush, green, red, tan, black, blue, and lavender.

She forgives him. Chameleons are changelings after all. Who really wants to be a 9 to 5 lizard day after day? The lizard boy is fed up with the madness of a world that would steal the youthful love of eager lizards and whisk their energy into the human trades. Hence his incontinence, his wetting himself, his leap out into the street with arms waving. Wise lover lizards take siesta from the high noon desert sun. They retreat to their lizard holes to stave off the brutal heat. And sleep together on a cool smooth stone with tails entwined. Awake at dusk the couple steps out into the night to meet up with friends at the Cactus Bar. They laugh and dance, high on the sweet smell of the blooming brown-foot.

And then back home before the sun hits the doormat. A day of work. Games played. Bellies full. A smooth stone bed where two lizard spoons sleep contented into the hot day.

Thanks again for the canvases Dan. Back to the painting board. See you tonight at the Cactus Bar.

I Show Off My Incontinence Because I Love You 2014.
Acrylic on hard board 11X 14"

Oswego Is A Good Place To Fail

Wow. Yesterday I read a 2004 article on Roy Lichtenstein, a very famous painter of the late twentieth century. I already knew that he taught for several semesters at the state college in Oswego. I also read in a biography that his wife hated it here. The winters were tough and she began to drink like a fish. But I never knew what a great failure Lichtenstein was the day before he started painting comics for rich people. He was a novice abstract painter who loved Picasso and Cézanne. His paintings amassed unsold in the home studio.

I read with laughing eyes the early story of Roy. The parallels are enough to keep me plugging away at my own failure. I quote at length.

"Roy would say, 'I know any minute someone's going to come and shake me and say, Mr. Lichtenstein, it's time for your pills, and I'll be back in Oswego, in a wheelchair.' There was a touch of Lichtenstein's characteristic self-deprecating humour about that. But also a sense that he had been, as she says, 'very lucky to have been where he was at a given moment'".

Roy knew, like many painters do, that success is a crap shoot with a 1,679,616-sided die. Only a wise, self-deprecating Oswego artist would admit to this.

"But the teaching post he held in Oswego from 1957 to 1960 was a low point of his career, very far from the wealth and art stardom that were his within a couple of years... At the time he got the job in Oswego, Lichtenstein had been working as a painter for nearly 20 years, and achieved almost no success. Bruce Breland, a colleague of the time, remembered that Lichtenstein 'had shown in New York — with no results. He was showing paintings and they were going stone-nowhere.'"

All my paintings also going cement-nowhere in the basement.

"Lichtenstein did a series of part-time jobs — window dresser, draftsman, furniture designer, painting dials on instruments — while his wife, a successful interior designer, was the main breadwinner. Lee Csuri, sculptor and wife of another old friend, remembered that in the mid-1950s, 'Roy was very despondent about what he was doing. And feeling he was nowhere. His painting of that time was abstract expressionist, but it was very muddy'".

Yahoo! My wife is a graphic designer, the bread winner, and my feelings of despondency on a good day have me yank off just enough mustache nose hairs to goad me to the next chore.

"Then in 1957, he got the job in Oswego. But as Avis Berman, a researcher into Lichtenstein's life, concluded: 'Living in Oswego was disastrous for the Lichtensteins. The winters were brutal and Isabel lacked fulfilling work, and began drinking in earnest.' So at 37, Lichtenstein had a dead-end post in the sticks, a wife who was rapidly becoming an alcoholic, and a studio full of paintings no one wanted to look at. Then his luck began to change."

Oooh, I can only hope.

"As Dorothy Lichtenstein tells the story, 'Roy was always trying to get back to the New York area, and in 1960 he was able to get a job teaching at Rutgers University in New Jersey. And there was a group of interesting and lively people there, including the artists Alan Kaprow and George Segal. Roy had a feeling that if he'd still had a job teaching out in the boondocks, he might have done his first Pop work, but not carried on. He felt there was something that comes from response and encouragement that fuels you to go further than you might in a vacuum.'"

Response and encouragement. Roy had a feeling. Ron has one from time to time. He expresses it, and in return receives the appreciative song from a cricket stowing away beneath a cellar stair.

"But there might have been another trigger. As Chuck Csuri, Lee's husband, recalls, Lichtenstein's son David came home one day from school and complained: 'Joey's father's a policeman, and Henry's father's this, and Virginia's does that. And you're an artist and you can't draw.' Roy said, 'Oh, OK.' So he got out a canvas and drew a comic-book image. The result might have been *Look Mickey*, with Donald Duck and Mickey Mouse. In it, Donald is fishing, and says, 'Look Mickey, I've hooked a big one'. And a big, new idea was exactly what Lichtenstein had got hold of himself'".

That is all the parallel I need. Back in 1998 Roy's spirit must have hightailed it back to Oswego, and flew up my nose.

Now to focus on the work and the big break which is sure to come at fifty, using the logic of arrested development afflicting the middle-aged in the 21st century. I shall keep at work, seek escape, and let my mustache hairs grow into my mouth.

If I Was Mao, I'd Stop All The Plumbing In Manahatta 2014.
Acrylic on canvas 18 X 24"

Lock 'Em Up!

I think it's time to imprison Washington D.C.

Wire a 100,000 volt invisible fence around the perimeter wide enough to include the nasty parts of Virginia and Maryland. How do the imbeciles of our capital keep at it, day after day? Why do they? For nice aftershave? Is that it? Is it all about a Georgetown perfumery where Senator Feinstein or Dutch Ruppersberger shop for scent products? I know the feeling of self-edification. As a boy on Christmas mornings of the past I would get all dressed up in my new clothes boxed under the tree and take my annual alternating gift of department store Brut® or Old Spice® grooming products into the bathroom. I would clip my fingernails, shave the score of hairs off my face, button the cuffs of my sleeves, and drench myself in the scent of man. As a thirteen year old boy laying down beside the presents stacked under the tree I began to imagine Ron Throop to be a successful businessman and/or starting quarterback for the Miami Dolphins. That dreaming would dull as soon as thoughts of Simone Beretti popped into my head. She was the smart girl who sat in front of me in Mr. Swan's U.S. History class. She came with her smells too, and on Christmas morning recent memories of them mixed in with my cologne's superpower, had me daydream a future winter morning taking Simone for a ride on my Ski-doo® snowmobile. I would seat her in front so she couldn't fall off. I would protect her. And all would be right with the world.

Now I think of the teenage boy and girl Ron and Simone in 2018 with smart phones. I would be connected to nfl.com, and Simone to some cool Indie band website her older sister got her turned on to. We might sneak in a cryptic puppy love text from time to time, her calling me a "druggie" (I was not and am not), and me pointing out her uneven pony tail in class. We would put away the phones at our respective homes that night. Then Simone to her homework and me to *The Muppet Show,* and finally dragging my feet to some algebra I could not understand.

Larry Purvis was a fellow student at the time, a bully, but of another sort. A loner. He was a bit roly-poly with fat pink cheeks and blonde greasy hair. Kids shied away from him because rumor had it that he was a slimy pervert. There were tales about Larry getting caught playing doctor with very young girls and boys on his street, and that was such a foreign idea to the rest of us seventh and eight graders, so undeniably off-scene to pubescent teens, that it was a no-brainer to avoid Larry at every opportunity—in the halls, at lunch, but most definitely in the locker room.

Well, it turned out, according to my hometown friend and professional prison guard Pat, that today Larry wears a GPS ankle bracelet. The rumors were true. Larry is a convicted child predator and molester. Bound to be one growing in every school district I suppose.

Now I think of the peeping Toms at the N.S.A.* (and also members of Congress*, the President*, and any judge alive who enables them) intercepting the flirtations of our children, and I call for their arrest and imprisonment, and upon release made to wear an ankle bracelet for the rest of their lives, just like Larry Purvis. I think of the ubiquitous photo the media displays of the N.S.A.* headquarters, and now realize that every car's owner in that immense parking lot is a free Larry Purvis of America. Each one is drooling in on the privates of our children. Having not yet quit in shame is proof that the typical N.S.A.* employee is guilty and seeks strength in numbers of other perverts to shelter him or her self from the storm, the vitriolic type, released by parents of victimized children who, upon hearing news of the spying on little Suzie through the bathroom window, find themselves igniting mob torches in the night to hunt down a disgusting Larry Purvis.

Who wants their country to be run by peeping Toms and Thomasinas? Even the President's wife* will not slap his face in front of their boy and call him a "sick pig".

She must love her Chanel No. 5* too. Makes her feel important as 1st Lady pervert-enabler.

Don't Worry, I Can Throw A Cat Through The Clouds 2014. Acrylic on canvas 72 X 54"

Aeon Magazine

A friend of mine linked an article published in Aeon Magazine entitled "Is It OK To Make Art?: If You Express Your Creativity While Other People Go Hungry, You're Probably Not Making the World a Better Place". It argues partially for Effective Altruism, an activist movement to lighten world human and animal suffering. Please read it if you have the time. I have neither the patience nor kindness to deal with the upper crust when they get all high falutin' with another save the world guilt-arrogance complex.
http://aeon.co/magazine/philosophy/art-is-a-selfish-waste-of-time-says-effective-altruism/
The most sure fire way for an effective altruist to do good for others is immediate suicide, a hidden one, so no resources are used to humanely dispose of the body. Feed the worms so the soil is enriched and the next tree grows to suck in enough CO2 to offset the altruist's lifelong Pringle intake (He's had 343,242 up to last count). The effective altruist has an argument: Make a lot money and donate 10% to a "good" cause. Otherwise you are bad, because money is good. It got us antibiotics, global warming and nuclear weapons. Artists are poor, that means uselessly narcissistic I guess, and wholly uninterested in securing potable water to millions of suffering humanoids. That's right. Because of well-fed Western artists, children in Africa suffer terrible diseases. How dare those painters subsist on rice and beans when they can go corporate and sell toothpaste for Proctor and Gamble. Who do they think they are having all of that self-degradation fun for themselves! Everyone knows that in the West, the ends always justify the means. Become a high paid software engineer, and quit your day-longing, aspiring ceramist. You suck! You are a debauched human being. Go back to college and study whatever will make you the most disgusting carbon belcher in the world, just so long as 10% of your filth donates the ability for non-profits to distribute their help to the poor, of course after covering the high costs for all those overpaid positions at the institute. Apply for work at Lockheed Martin. Help develop a program to better drone angry poor families out of the way so Joe Merck researcher can walk freely through the rainforest without a poison dart aimed at his ass.

My God, now the little dandys want to take away the poor man's happiest joys—art! Why? Because it doesn't feed enough children in Somalia, or as the article smartly put it, "de-worm them". I read the article, felt a prick of shame, and then wrote back to my friend, "Thank goodness I'm a misanthrope". And boy am I! Western high standard of living! Did it ever occur to these effective altruists (AKA: over-educated elitist gobs) that families in Somalia might not want to have their children de-wormed? Or, okay, "de-worm us," they say, "but get your dirty electricity out of our faces!" Maybe the poor third-worlders don't want another pallet of Western medicine dropped on their reserva-I mean, villages. Maybe their idea of childhood disease is similar to one felt by a mama black bear and her cubs. Maybe death is life and vice-versa. Maybe not. Maybe families would rather starve than live the Western life of constipated ennui birthing more effective altruists to fly all over the earth thinking funny money is savior for everyone. Maybe not. Maybe I am way off.

Maybe third-worlders prefer worms as an unhappy but necessary alternative to Western type 2 diabetes, asthma, heart disease, stroke, obesity, hypertension, cancer, alcoholism, street drug addiction, pharmaceutical drug addiction, suicidal and homicidal tendencies, gout, depression, and E.A.D. (effective altruist disease), to name a few Western lovelies we shall receive for making all of that glorious money in order to cover the guilt of our social dysfunction.

Making creative, dreamy people guilty for making art. Must be a CIA initiative. Yes, the CIA. Why not? It's undisclosed multi-billion dollar budget alone could feed and de-worm the world, and at the same time terrorize less people wearing loincloths. Maybe the effective altruists can find courage to lambaste the secret killers, or make enough dreamy artist-folks focus their creative attention on "shame art" to eliminate the secret killer society once and for all. Imagine all of that money freed up for the benefit of degraded non-Western society. A better plan I think than telling Western poor people with paintbrushes and a pot of beans soaking on the stove that they just think too highly of themselves to do any good for the world. They should feel bad for having a flush toilet and an available reservoir of chemical water to hydrate themselves. Love those soldiers though, paid killers, politicians, jingoes, judges, Presidents of Western nations, the latter who literally have overnight power to de-worm unhappy children with intestinal ache. But do they wield it? No. Why? Because their love of power does not encompass suffering children. Probably the only people outside of the tremendous brain trust of the effective altruists who would ever call on a leader to feed the world, are the artists. So the solution presented by the altruist, using the always faultless logic of the elitist, is to guilt the artists into seeking gobs and gobs of money, in order to feed an already monstrously arrogant Western culture on the brink of extinction.

Antilogic.

Finally, for the love of the suffering hordes of humanity, how much does this de-worming medicine cost? Are the effective altruists citing retail, wholesale, or the bare bones investment to manufacture one pill to free a child of her tummy cramps, while demanding that painters stop painting to save the world? They are aware, yes, holed up in their peaceful suburban think tank, that one year's profits from several leading pharmaceutical companies could probably de-worm, feed, clothe and educate collegiately all the poor children of the world? That maybe the capitalist-fascist system that awards company heads at GlaxoSmithKline the wealth of Croesus is what actually kills innocent babies across every wasteland on earth. Maybe a future altruist bio-chemist like Alexander Fleming is who children of the world need, and not a hapless painter who has been known to acquire in a lifetime not much more money than a penny fountain at the zoo. Maybe this new age Fleming could also be trained to go all commando, kidnap a Big Pharma CEO, and torture him politely once for every dollar he hoards for himself and other stinking gut rot members of the good ole boy's club.

Medicine is made. The food can be distributed. At my state fair a couple years back, the national guard had an exhibit proudly displaying their crowd control grenade launcher. Two hundred explosives released in one second at politically incorrect crowds. Upon detonation each mini-bomb sent super sharp shrapnel to finish the job if the concussion and burning didn't mutilate all the bystanders first. How much does the typical effective altruist think one of these machines cost Western society? I mean, above the bottom line of another painter's "pretty picture"? We need to make a profit here, remember? That's right. I can become a soldier. There. Now that's some regular pay. And 10% of that is 100% more than I have ever profited by creative effort. What a narcissistic tool I am. I could be operating a drone in Nevada, one to annihilate the next Somalian wedding party. At least then I'd be doing my part as a human being. Acting on a guilt pledge to feed the world, giving up another useless painting to have lunch with the great altruist thinkers of the world.

I have a solution, even if it develops into a parallel dystopian future the altruists advocate with their "ends justify the means" trash talk. It is this: Eliminate the distributor, whether it be armies or pharmacies, and kick an altruist where it hurts for being such a god damn sissy to power. We know who is guilty.

And it's never ever the poor; no matter how rich they are.

Rose Dreams Bavaria With Spirit Cat 2014.
Acrylic on canvas 18 X 24"

Rose Dreams Bavaria With Spirit Cat

If there is a wealthy Bavarian with a guest cottage, please consider hiring me for the summer. I will paint your Alps. Every one. All the flora and fauna too. And you can keep the canvases to sell to your contacts in Munich during the autumn rains. I have a wife and child in my charge. I will worry about their board, provided that you board me extravagantly. I will share my hams and cakes with them and paint the Danube down to the last lucky salmon. Tramping your forest in dream at dawn and dusk… Breathing in the mountain air so deep that the tips of my toes expand and release with enthusiastic mirth. I'll need a room that can get messy, materials, and cheerful encouragement. I want your wife to be an elder Gretel who is maternal yet still dreaming like the child a confectionery cottage. We will spread the witches' ashes at the base of the elder bush to level the soil pH, and work all day like the peasant I am and always will be until the first yodel of sunset hushes the song of the yellowhammer. We shall be a healthy burden no more the morning the elderberry has ripened to black purple.

What an affordable way to acquire several Throops for your collection. Paintings with you and your family in mind. A real connection. Have the maid air the place out in late May. Let me know as soon as possible the exact date to arrive. I need to plan and secure a passport for the girls.

These Nights Light An Oyster Cracker Moon Over A Red Tide Chowder
2014. Acrylic on canvas 18 X 24"

Oyster Cracker Moon Over A Red Tide Chowder

This morning I shall feed two birds with one oyster cracker. The following vignette recounts a past Christmas season when I went out peddling my own books. My wife and I had a twelve-year old and a yearling to wow with Christmas gifts, but neither dime nor dollar in the money bowl. Yesterday we received another solicitation from Chase in the mail telling us to open a checking account with their bank. They will deposit $200.00 as a free gift. That is one hell of an oyster cracker!

Chase, Inc. as door to door salesman. Peddling other people's money, gobs of it, for some nefarious reason of which we can only guess. "Here's 200 clams. Not a painting. No book to read. Direct deposit with us and you'll be able to stuff a whole tub with oyster crackers." Why their offer grinds at my insides, I don't know. Perhaps my success at repetitive failure from hawking creative writing and painting has finally caught up with my mortal pride. Yesterday I wrote about how local artists everywhere need to boycott galleries, museums, any third party advocates who claim the secret knowledge of appraising art for the people. They have taken away our right to peddle, to personalize, to self-portraiture. The middlemen of art have taught the people to beware of the unrepresented artist. He can't have anything you want. He's up to no good, and lacking any real talent, we can assure you…

I need to connect to people. I don't want Rita the gallerist in my life. Rita needs Rita and the painter gives a piece of himself to Rita to help Rita find Rita. How much is that worth? Not a penny more than a gifted $200.00 deposit and a new pleather checkbook from the galleries of JP Morgan Chase. Hurry, this offer wont's last. We'll hold death's door open to the working class, but only for a limited time.

We will turn down Chase's money offer. The company will not suffer. No top executive will marvel at the surprisingly high cost of rope at his neighborhood home center after bombing another marketing plan. I will never again peddle my books to the middleman. He is just that. A "middle" man. Keeping the "low" low. False praising the "high" highly. The middle secures more antidepressants, and easy admittance into the chowder house of our choice. Hence the previous painting and the following story:

Rather Have An Oyster Cracker?

Two thousand-thirty-five years ago Christ was born in the land
without snow. He was a dark-haired baby who didn't wear diapers.
Christ was a baby and all babies live peace. Besides hitting his
mother when he wanted her to play with him, he was very peaceful. Kings brought the divine child presents, not one of them a
small plastic toy phone. A variety of presents, but not one that a
child would want to play with. Frankincense and Mir? Don't ask.
Just receive and smile, smile and receive, and make sure the gifts
are big enough not to get lodged in your new savior's throat.

This Christmas more than one person will drive forty miles to
purchase a popular candle holder. When my oldest daughter was
very young, she was taught to give nothing besides love and attention, and occasional crayon drawings of devotion. Slowly, grad-
ually, over the past couple years, Santa Claus has left her heart. It
is only a matter of time before Christmas makes her deeply and
hopelessly frazzled like the rest of us.

I am out of the kind of work that writes you a check for the
holidays. Joy has left my body. I have no way of knowing if I will
ever be able to help support this family financially. And because
of the money problem, I start to wonder if I am husband or father,
or anything good at all. Money is the sickness of our hearts. It
is the sole cause of any depression that exists where no tragedy
has occurred. Because of money I did something yesterday that I
thought I would never do. I went out peddling my books all over
three counties. I took a day to do it. I had to ask my wife to take off
from work. I borrowed a car. It had an American flag attached out
the back window waving "I am tasteless" to all and sundry on a
cold, bright December morning.

I drove to every bookstore and library in Central New York. By
the end of the day I sold to three stores and involuntarily donated
one set to a library. I walked up to the head librarian embracing
my precious books. He received me quite cordially. I expected him
to escort me over to the money box and pay me for my efforts.
Patiently I waited while he talked about the lack of arts and
culture in the Mohawk Valley. "One bookstore," he complained,
"in a county of 250,000. Can you believe it?" Yes I thought, but
here, let me put my hand out again, palm up, and hope that you

get the hint. Nothing. Instead he stepped into his office and came out grasping the local swap sheet, suggesting that I advertise my books with the used cars. Then he offered me a book signing, but recanted, saying that in the past those only worked well with children's book authors. Then I imagined that he would prefer to ram the heel of his boot against my skull rather than pay me the paltry sum necessary to justify my existence as a writer. Culture or no culture. I should have killed him on the spot and fished through the petty cash box myself.

Now the thought of peddling my own books was and is a personal nightmare. Total desperation made me do it. Man will succumb to anything when the money is tight enough to cheat his own children. Except work at a dollar store. No. I won't do that. So what if an offer has already been made...? No. I will very calmly open up an artery before dehumanizing my existence at a dollar store.

After a day driving in and around Syracuse New York, I discovered the worst hole in all of the world to raise a sane family. You drive around for a full morning in it, penniless, in a borrowed car and see for yourself what an incurably sick and twisted, groaning hell of a city it is. Two of the bookstores on my list of ten were abandoned. Two more sold only pornography. Two were consignment, and the second one of these wouldn't take my books unless he could get the whole set for fifteen cents.

Yesterday I lived the life of a traveling salesman in America. Except I was selling a product which I made myself. Of course one couldn't eat my product—strike one. Nor was it something quite like holly leaf wrapping paper sold at a huge profit for charity. Strike two. Encyclopedias might have brought better luck, if I went door-to-door with the volumes I researched, wrote and published myself. Strike three and out. Actually lying prone in a basement beside a gassed Willy Loman.

A few years ago my chef left the restaurant business to peddle oyster crackers for an upstart company. Up before dawn, he drove his car over two hundred miles every day except Sunday. Boxes of light, airy oyster crackers stacked to the ceiling in the back seat. He peddled throughout a retail world that he convinced himself was in sufficient need of better oyster crackers. The best oyster crackers. In fact, over time, he couldn't understand how restaurants stayed in business without his delicious oyster crackers in stock.

Once he got me to try them, while he stood at my side waiting for affirmation. Holy God, the blind arrogance of delusion! Every time he said "oyster cracker" I envisioned spiraling rounds of slow-motion bullets busting out the back of my skull. His behavior was beyond delusional. It was insane, maniacal—an oyster cracker... Jesus Christ! Yet I played along, chewing for his benefit, although at the time I felt like striking him down and stuffing his mouth full of oyster crackers. He wanted to sell them to everyone. He was preaching the Word about oyster crackers. Each book that I wrote and got published, no matter what value its content, was written with the dreams that appear while walking alone at night in fear of death. I collaborated and created with the body which houses my soul. It was all that I had then, and all I have now. For $12.95 I will share its story with you. That's all the Word I know.

You say sure? As long as it's told over a bowl of steaming hot seafood chowder? Fine. Just try to ignore the steady stream of bullets drilling holes into my head. Promise me you'll crush those crackers quickly and take the soup onto your lap. I'm spilling blood.

Why this staunch, masochistic refusal to become equally excited over my own creations? How can man live a whole life never to stand up and lustily sing his own praises? Even if he foolishly sings to some greater power beyond him... It has got to be more stimulating than worshiping oyster crackers, right? I mean, how could my old boss become the apostle of a dry cracker company without having committed suicide yet? Hasn't he already gone way beyond the point of just considering it? Unless the crackers are laced with enough extra preservatives to fool the rest of us into thinking that he lives, I tell you that he must be dead already. A soul must die each moment an oyster cracker gets believed in.

To tell the truth, I hate my books. I despise them. I hate the product that I wanted to sell yesterday, during a weak moment when I thought my children needed toys for Christmas.

Privately, however, I intend to sing my praises while the rest of mankind watches me bleed. But I won't be singing for your money. I will sing, but know that I know it's not what I write into books that makes me praise-worthy. I am 100% man. I am a man. My blood heats up my wonder and desire. I can be squeezed until warm blood spurts out of my pours. But I will continue to sing while bleeding. I believe that every man's blood is my own blood. And every man should sing the song of watching it flow. I am singing for me and for you, even if I know that you, if given the choice, would choose a low-sodium oyster cracker over the intactness of my blood and its systems. Translated into easy, easy easy...

You suck
my blood.
But would rather have an oyster cracker.

Your Institutional Job Helped Craft A Fool My Love Chum
2014. Acrylic on canvas 24 X 32"

Harvest Moon 2014. Acrylic on canvas 18 X 24"

Harvest Moon

This one began yesterday morning as another reaction to Wednesday's blizzard. I wanted a sun that came up from the sea ready to UV my brain stem boiled lobster red. At 10:00 a.m. I had it with winter, staring out my window at the gray, white, black, brown stained ugh-blah of dormancy. Yellow. Slap! Schlop! Lots of it. Red, a gob-a-bob. Some pathetic bird, and then pop! Neil Young's masterpiece "Harvest Moon" at noon. Like a door thrown open in my brain, and a push from behind into a room called "What Matters". A bed made up for my hibernating sweetheart and me. A safe home for the children. Dandelions and lavender bees. My little girls chasing rabbits and squirrels. Another trip around the sun. So in love and luck with my lifelong friend. Close the door. Real spring is a month away. Take the time for wine and rest and memory. Let the gray heartache feed off the final slab of November fat. Think on the moon of October, when you welcomed winter with warm love, not the fighting cock reaction of a man pinned down by a desperate March.

The secret of happiness? Time to think like Neil Young did back in 1993. A made up musical poem of five minutes that can teach more about love, longing, and tenderness than all the libraries of the Internet universe ever will. Brand that learning onto your cranium wall, and then move on to the next subject...

Getting our butts down to Florida for an ocean breeze walk next winter, no matter what the cost.

Mr. Picasso, By December I Will Have Baked 9 Apple Pies and 3 Crisps 2014.
Acrylic on canvas 24 X 18"

Art Criticism

I just finished reading an article about cronyism in art and culture. It provided rare admission on a subject that many unfunded artists know in their hearts to be all too true. The business of art is anti-art. The "good ole boys" club. Paid administrators (curators, gallerists, art faculty) seeking non-paid visual artists who, by virtue of "poverty in the arts", are forced to either request admission into the club or schlepp a scam they hope will convince the right paid people. Art is defeated on a mass scale. It has become another corporate model, open to collectivism and always in danger of cronyism. No snake-oil salesman ever fell in love with snake oil first and then sought distribution of, not just an imperfection, but also a worthless placebo that only the ignorant believed had merit. On the contrary, the salesman was always a desperate working man seeking pride with a job while struggling with a family in a muck-stagnant economy. It was the snake-oil company that placed adds in farmland newspapers enticing the poor to hawk to the poor a product said to improve health and wellness. The company knew what it was up to. Likewise, the art industry plays the same game claiming to have a soothing syrup for the people's mental health. The museum, established gallery, PhD, multimillion dollar "auction" house, and the billionaire all claiming to possess gnostic insight to the mysteries of art. They have no freaking idea what art is any more than I do, or the article's author, or kangaroos in Australia.

Picasso and Dali were once household names while they lived. And then Pollock and de Kooning, to name a few. The corporate model had not yet fully "metastasized" into the art world. These artists and others were cherry-picked by influential people and so big media (already well-established) latched on to their individual stories because big media schmoozed at weekend parties with the influential people. Still, the corporate cancer persisted, as it always will. Kellog's Corn Flakes added more sugar to the same wet, chewed-like mush twice-baked, added a playful type, and a tiger for a mascot. Voila! *Frosted Flakes*. The corporate paradigm of the 1960's and beyond. "The Depression generation brought you Picasso. We give you Warhol. Next, to cement our complete control of an industry, we printed the word "organic" on our cereals, and, to certify the illusion of self-liberation, here is the shiny new pervert Jeff Koons hosting a company of college grads in a Manhattan factory to sculpt many replicas of his penis for you!"

Picasso was a household name because big business, in all of its post-war glory, via the voices of politicians and media, needed to pretend instant sophistication to match its multinational approach to schlepping snake oil around the globe. In one famous experiment, Stanley Milgram proved to the powers that be that control is a breeze. Just give someone a title and a white coat, and kids will follow orders to shoot and kill other kids half a world away. Likewise, starving artists will enter a lottery their whole lives and hope to be authenticated. The new economy spewed more and more lower and middle class kids with art degrees, but lacking the courage to pursue an actual career in expression. Hence the lackeys of art business. The snake oil salespeople. The army of art history professionals getting tenured jobs in corporate universities. They were not to blame. They were folks with families in need of love and care. No criticism would ever be allowed in to undermine their careers as long as there was a living to be had. To them, by virtue of economic survival, art became money. Powerful art administrators not only peddled the snake oil, but controlled the ranks of its production and distribution. But it was never their art to become money in the first place.

There are solutions to cronyism. They can be found wherever art is alive and needs to be nurtured.

Eliminate the middle man. Boycott all third party galleries and museums. From the dinosaur downtown to the humble subsidized gallery at the state college. Take away the eyes and judgment of the third party. Make art for the patron once again. Let them create personal hobbies looking for their own concept of "the diamond in the rough". Have a show in your living room. Pool monies with artist friends and rent an abandoned gallery for a month. Get back the time you lost trying to impress the gallerist or curator who judged your snake oil by its packaging, its reviews on Amazon, or the accolades on a CV (Latin for "current viability").

Find the coffee house in your hometown to meet and socialize with other artists to talk about everything. This is a top priority. The business of art fears the merger of artists. Their congruence is its downfall.

To stress how unlocal artists are in my tiny town, I give you the example of our state university art department. The combined art education of the faculty is over 200 years. According to the industrial system, they are recognized, real, credentialed, and of course, paid living artists. They disseminate the knowledge and skills acquired, and are successful in that young people still graduate knowing how to draw a chair and place historical artists into their proper movement. That is their day job. But at night the professors return home, the full timers to the suburbs, the adjuncts to a second job, and then finally to a rented apartment in town. If one ever has a show, a piece or two gets entered in the annual faculty exhibition, or representation is sought in his off time anywhere outside of our small city. At the university, the adjunct suffers second class citizenship, even if his pencil drawing of a tree looks a spark better than the same tree drawn by the full professor. The oneupmanship begets avarice. Avarice begets competition. And competition in art breeds pettiness. So my small city becomes just another "Hey Spike" to the Great bulldogs New York and Los Angeles who have practically eliminated all that was ever good about art, that is, its expressive communication to known human beings. Art in America is the NFL, and no longer a touch football game in the park with Howard, the art history professor, Rita, the painter, and Robert the sculptor, to name a few of the creatives who get together after work for team sports and then later, a beer. To make matters worse, visiting artists are brought in from around the country to "inspire" the students. Yet the students never see the corporate business model which delivered the talented anomaly from New York City—The secret art agent, nor the international C.V. which puts in writing how amazing this guy's psychedelic paper mache paper wasp's nests truly are. Believe it. The MoMA said so. Buy him.

I will spend this week posting criticisms and solutions to replace the corporate paradigm with plans I believe are better suited to the career happiness of the individual man and woman as artist. No matter where we live, we all are local. The minions running the business of art would prefer we all be loco, separated, howling at the moon, and crushing the fingers of potential friends and colleagues on the ladder of success, always brought to you by a lower humanity seeking your work to bring them to the top.

Lemons And Lavender 2014. Acrylic on canvas 48 X 36"

Sex Education In Schools Has My Heart Fill Up With Water

My thirteen year old daughter got to pass around a condom in class yesterday with classmates. Her friend Ken learned a new word: "ejaculation". And the eleven-year old giggler sitting next to her can now identify an erect penis. They are being taught "safe sex" by a team of outsiders who visit her school four times a year (twice in fall, twice in spring) to show the children how to have safe sex.

No doubt about it, the Puritans still scour our rotten souls. Are there any other mandated "health" education subjects I need to know about? The state keeps pushing the sex one. We get it. AIDS. Unwanted pregnancy. Yes, bad, scary. So is decapitation in a Chevy Cruze, yet I'm sure legislators do not feel the political pressure to mandate driver education to my thirteen-year old, even if she finds herself drooling for sex in the passenger seat of a car this summer, and the car driver rolls the car over a cliff while cleaning up his ejaculation. What about the threat of Type 2 diabetes and the traveling pedagogic team of Safe Eaters? They leap into class carrying baskets of fresh fruits and vegetables. The kids shoot carrot stick darts at posters bearing the smug mugs of Kraft and General Mills CEO's.

No, according to our state and federal education departments, half her class is rolling around in bed, licking the dust out of Dorito bags and dreaming of unprotected sex. Rebel teens and preteens. Anne of the Green Gables had to worry about sex too. Gilbert was ready, but not for syphilis. Matthew had Anne alone in the pig barn too often, and Marilla, with the political push of the women's rotary, was able to persuade the teacher to speak about farmer pedophilia, and the smutty culture practiced by Canadian cows out twerking in the field. Anne and Gilbert courted in college and probably fooled around a bit, and I am certain they had unprotected sex, but probably not with the whole fraternity and likewise, sorority. Just one of those silly traditions from way back when—sex with one you love, or at least, are determined to marry. Still, there was always a risk, even with just the one partner. A shotgun wedding and a private shame suffered by the family.

What else, beside STD's, do our little children need to learn by

strangers in this cowardly new world? I mentioned safe driving.
Perhaps they should wear little condom helmets so, after the head
slams against the dash, the tainted blood doesn't freely pour out
of an ear potentially infecting the other passengers. Instruction
in vigilant hand washing and a mild electric shock at the shared
drinking fountain could weaken flu outbreaks, and prevent a few
rotavirus accidents in the kid's new jeans. Banning the marine
recruiter from the guidance office might save one or two young
girls from guaranteed sexual humiliation. We could always do
the near impossible, and get these kids taught a civics lesson by a
competent civics teacher, one who has read his nation's constitution, and can interpret the Bill of Rights in the same liberal way it
was meant to be interpreted by war weary white guys wanting to
check future abuse of power. That is, in the liberal sense that each
of us has a right to practice the freedoms guaranteed by the first
ten amendments. We have the freedom of speech but not to yell
"fire" in a crowded auditorium. Likewise, I have the freedom to
talk with my daughter about the birds and the bees, but would be
arrested on the spot should I walk into a school displaying a picture of an erect penis for all and sundry. According to that dying,
old-fashioned document The U.S. Constitution, I still reserve the
right to protest "professionals" being granted the legal opportunity
to show kids the same penis.

　All joking aside. Perhaps I am one of those few parents left in
America still having meaningful conversations with his child.
Maybe I know too much since my daughter, as a private human
being, came through the door upset that her teachers want her to
know not only what an erection is, but what to do with it when it
appears out of the blue. She told me that she was not ready for that
information. She didn't want a condom put into her hand. She
knew what her vagina looked like. She didn't want Ken to know
what her vagina looked like. Not yet anyway. Not until her heart
got brave enough to hold his hand. I feel that she has been violated.
If her uncle Bob got caught telling these stories to her, Uncle Bob
would go to jail. At least Uncle Bob is my brother. It would be up
to me to give him my permission on what I believe is a sensitive
subject for girls and boys two years older from believing in Santa.
Not because it shouldn't be taught. It should. But not to pre or
mid-pubescent children. Not by Uncle Bob, and certainly not by

the state traveling safe-sex team.

It is our responsibility as procreating adults to decide when our children are ready for the state version of sex education. We are a liberal family with an old-fashioned, conservative approach to raising children. I object to the state normalizing casual sex to keep up with Hollywood and other cheesy media executives who, by virtue of their chosen careers, take a lizard's approach to bringing up the kids. We are liberal. Not in the Hollywood liberal way, which is just more of the same greasy smut smeared on a smooth arrow. It's projected trajectory will land us all in looney land soon enough. Love and nurturing do not rise in proportion to cultural degeneration. It's obvious to anyone who loves. It is degenerate to show kids sex before they're even thinking of it. Even Hollywood rates its smut so we as parents can decide if it's smut worth sharing with our only angels.

The 2014 Oscar Ceremonial Attendees

The class gulf is wide. Our own neighbors and friends uninsured, or at best underinsured. And yet drone technology advanced and invested in. A chauffeur for your senator. A no-bid
contract for Haliburton to help mop up the human suffering in
Iraq. Prescribed fish oil Lovaza is for the entitled at $240.00 for
a one month supply. GlaxoSmithKline used a golden blender to
mutilate its catch from the North Sea. Lucky for me my wife is
powerfully insured. So I get it for ten dollars. I have an extra ten
years to live because she was at the right place at the right time
when landing the only graphic design job with benefits in a thirty
mile radius. Twenty years ago fish oil was quack. Now it's prescribed. Drops triglycerides, staves off pancreatitis. Of course only
the Lovaza is concentrated with 1000 squeezed and wrung out
fish per capsule. The stuff in the grocery store isn't as potent, and
without expert medical counsel, who would know which type of
diabetes to expect with the cheaper choice anyway?

We cannot afford this culture anymore. Turn off the radio, the
television, the major "newspaper" on the Internet. Yesterday the
latter prescribed to the elite of planet earth (Hollywood actors at
the Oscars), in order to get more "hits" so Lockheed Martin and
Kraft mayonnaise will advertise with it. It was a twitter photo of
the healthy and insured laughing in the know that no one they
love or like shall ever need for basic care. I watched the Red Carpet
pre-Oscar with some friends and alluded to the sham that is the
Oscar ceremony. The producers do their best to show the world
these scripted humanoids as folks appearing just like themselves
on television. The viewers at home don't see the army of personal
aids and body guards waiting beside black SUV's in the street. I
see them. I see my governor too spending our money on his hair
spray, the 10 mpg SUV, and sometimes, in moments of state crisis,
the trooper chopper trip to the latest online tragedy. I see the
waste, the avarice, the fear. I see Angelina Jolie having a double
mastectomy and a tanning session on the same day because she
can afford to be preemptive. Risk her career at any moment to
demand all women that opportunity NOW—ho boy. Never ever.

That is because we, as media denizens of planet earth, are unable to separate the good from the bad. But I will try.

The last good Oscar ceremony occurred way back in 2003 when Michael Moore accepted his award for best documentary, *Bowling For Columbine*; just a few days after our tax money was used to shock and awe (euphemism for "shrapnel inbed") other people's children several thousand miles away, Moore found the courage to speak out among a populace of fantastically immoral and ignorant human beings—not only the crowd of lowly actor Cro-magnon men and their tanned-cleavage women, but an entire nation of tuned-in bored and slothful enemies of its own species. Afterward, that audaciously talented, renaissance man sleazeball Steve Martin, boasted of his ability to act under pressure as MC and sweep under the rug our immense national shame—a wealthy American, Michael Moore, so illogically burdened with an invasive conscience.

Paddle-To-Com-Pla-Cen-Cy 2014. Acrylic on canvas 52 X 41"

Paddle-To-Com-Pla-Cen-Cy

Divide and conquer. Offer a new John Deere to my namby-Bambi warrior neighbor and why should he care if a speculum was affixed to the mouths of every child outside his six acres, and benzene poured down their gullible gullets? He got his new tractor. That's good enough for him. German Hans got to keep his assembly line job at the plant too back in '44 as long as he didn't complain about the chain gang of Polish slaves out in the steel yard. Outside his sleepy village a smokestack exhaled overtime a peculiar smell that only rumor could define, but thought better left unsaid. Anyway Christmas was coming, and that kind of horror exposed would dampen the children's spirits.

New York State is poised to allow massive injections of benzene into the subterranean world which encases our ground water. Sometimes art and politics must mix else we do nothing but order coffee, watch Netflix, and wait for the dirty urban trend-setters to inform us ignorant country mice on taste, ad nauseum.

The gas lobbyist knows this game well. Copied right out of the playbook of the coal and oil magnates. Bring the local idiot a six-pack. After the second beer start praising his ignorance. Say something like deer hunting is a man thing to do and only sissies would think about the purity of their drinking water. Get him to laugh about prejudice or bigotry, pretend rage at the "liberals" in Washington who want to regulate progress, tell him how much you admire his countryman thinking and of course global warming can't be true if it ever snows. Get out the contract. Tell him the money prize. Look how stern and concentrated his thoughts while signing his name with your leader's golden pen.

Thank him toughly. Get into your rented F350. Drive over to the hotel holding your stack of signed contracts. Dress into your oxford shirt and BMW. Turn on satellite radio, and drive back home to wife and kids whom you love deeply.

Back home to any German town 1944.

David The Talented 1942- 2012. Acrylic on canvas 16 X 20"

The Curators of the Smithsonian American Art Museum and Renwick Gallery Need A History Lesson

Two years ago I set out to document the genealogy of Throops, of which I am the last male in my line. During the Great Depression my Great Grandfather Henry made genealogy his wintertime hobby, when no work was available to an engineer building roads and bridges. He amassed quite an impressive archive to pass on. Old tin types and photos, letters from the mid-nineteenth century, his grandfather's handwritten autobiography, personal Civil War artifacts and stories handed down from his father, etc., etc. He was a born archivist, yet few in his circle of friends and family appreciated his side work, and boxes got stored in the attic over the course of three more generations. I took up his work in 2012, traveling to all the towns where the family settled since arriving to North America in 1660, and adding more detail to his archive, as well as a poet/painter's imagination in paint, prose, collage and modern home video technology. I painted 11 portraits of the male line, pasted an eight foot long collage of time line detail, edited a video of my odyssey, and published a colorful book on the patronym, all on my own dime. No grants, no special presents, no expectation of reward. I had a show in October of that year. Good friends came, a few acquaintances, and my begging jar made $130.00 cash for the hundreds of hours put into the display. The book was an absolute joy in the making. I had my father's handwriting made into a font and used it in many aspects of the design.

Here is a link to the movie on Vimeo:
http://vimeo.com/50577631.

In late 2013 I was corresponding with a representative of the Renwick Gallery about acquisition of this work. My intention was/ is to preserve in the American Painter archive my historical work as an American painter. At least there it would last as long as the United States remained a sovereign entity.

At first I was vying for a purchase of my work, but the assistant curator hinted that I should also offer it as donation to the museum. I agreed. My intention was/is mostly archival. I want my great grandchild to have access beyond the thermostatically uncontrolled attic of the future. The assistant agreed to pass the request over to the curatorial team. And I got my reply of "no thank you" by the end of the week.

Ho boy. Now for the argument in favor of nullification.

My wife and I pay a federal tax of about $4,000 a year, maybe more, probably more, but we figure like children in matters of finance. Many people we know have made a touch upon the government till at some point over the course of their lives. Veteran's benefits, disability checks, and recent Affordable Healthcare recipients to name a few. Many receive no benefit from paying federal tax, other than the illusory cover of protection from a military build up out of control. The Smithsonian is a subsidized institution, as are national parks, and federal highway programs. We pay our half-penny to curators in D.C. to oversee the archive of our history, and our 26th part of a penny to the overseers at the Renwick. Sure, my family can spend a couple thousand bucks visiting Washington D.C. and attend a full day in the Renwick for free, but it's not for free, as the capital makes its dime on our visit one way or another. In fact our stay in D.C actually helps authenticate a system that has become corrupt beyond recognition of its original intention. As a living American painter I believe my request to have the above work archived must be taken seriously. It is respectful payback for my yearly investment made to the coffers of this depleted nation. Just accepting a copy of the book for future reference would have been acceptable to me. A request from the last man in a Throop legacy dating all the way back to 1660 who also happens to be a professional painter! What excuse can the curators of the Renwick possibly give that is not grossly unfair as well as insulting? They represent an historical archive of American painters. How many alive today recently completed a thorough genealogy backed by individual portraits of each male member of eleven generations? My guess is zero, which gives me some justification to make a claim for storage at least, by virtue of American originality. The Renwick has a basement and the basement can possess a bookshelf to house a Throop publication. I never wanted a floor show. I just expect the art archivists to do their damn job. There is room. The burden is on the curators to prove the contrary. Otherwise, the pink slips. Even I, without doctoral training, would recognize a work of historical significance.

A relative Deborah Goldsmith has some work in the Renwick.

She painted several Throops in the Burned Over District of central New York in the early 19th century, making weekend portraits for a time before she married my Great Great Great cousin and then died young. She was a talented poet (my daughters and wife recite one of her poems in the video). There are about ten of her paintings surviving in museums around the country. Her work is very representative of an era in American history when no one graduated from universities as art curators. Valuable historical artifacts weren't compiled when the compiling mattered—when the work was fresh, available, and undamaged. Today we have multiple millions of dollars exchanged educating professional art archivists who act as if they have not learned a damn thing. They will let me die with a moldy basement stuffed to the ceiling of historically relevant yet significantly damaged lifetime build up of canvases. My children will contact an assistant curator at the Renwick to inquire about donating some of the work. Even then I think acceptance would be a toss-up. One has to be good and dead before a modern educated curator gets hit on the head with an understanding of historical significance. Maybe my great grandkids will have better luck. Maybe nobody in the line gets included in the American legacy. And then an old Whistler depicting a rabbit in the snow is found in someone's attic, and the $6,000 banners go up around the Renwick calling out to the tourists to come see another ubiquitous painter of our repetitive surface history, ad nauseum.

And so the subsidized bureaucracy in America feeds upon itself. What's new?

An Introduction to the Book That The Renwick Finds Unacceptable For Free

I remember the first time I got a hold of Throop/Goldsmith Ancestral Charts. My father had me borrow it, as well as Henry's three unpublished manuscripts (History, Charts, and Photos) when I was 26 years old. I leafed through the pages at my makeshift desk of early sorrows, while dreaming of Henry Miller, Thoreau, Whitman, Kenneth Patchen, etc. I was going to become them, not myself, which, in a fact I could not conceive of at the time, was all I ever was going to be. The study of genealogy is not for the modern twenty-something. It is a very rare wonder, a

young man or woman today delving into the world of their ancestors. Yet for Henry Throop it was an interest of his at an early age.
Was genealogy a popular pastime at the turn of the 20th century?
His book of local deaths, begun at age eleven, was most likely a
professional duty left by a recently deceased country doctor to
his son, and not a boy's macabre fascination to be diagnosed by
the Freudians of his day. Still Henry's interest in the families of
Lebanon, N.Y., even in his time, was probably a peculiar quirk
for a young man soon off to academy and then college. His early
journals are replete with accounts of local marriages, births and
deaths. In hindsight this sheds light to a different career path that
would have brought him uncommon joys. A successful engineer,
I have no doubt that Henry was a born historian. Maybe he would
have tossed into the ditch Macadam Road worries and transit
dreams, provided there existed an economy in his day that en-
couraged the intellectual flights of fancy of poor country boys.

So I returned the books to my Dad, giving back no more than
"Hmphh, imagine that!" out of the exchange, and continued on
my own path of raising a daughter half-time as a line cook in a
rinky-dink restaurant. I had dreams too. The literary life! A path
of writing out my history as it happened; in the modern fashion
a la´Henry Miller — the good, the bad, the private and often truly
embarrassing. Unlike my great grandfather, I actually lived in an
economy where I could choose any path I wanted, provided I paid
my dues to the university that would graduate me to the career
and/or income level of my choice. And yet unlike Henry I was
raised in a community that worshiped its own immediate marvel-
ousness and seemed to cut all ties to its past. It's funny how Henry
mentions with amusement in his autobiography that his children
Ronald and Robert thought he lived in "Bible" times. And yet I
think of my grandfather Ronald as the most conservative, traditional human being that ever walked the earth.

I am told by my father David that Ronald took little interest in
Henry's passion for the past. Yet I know now that by succumbing
to the power of tradition, Ronald proved to be quite gifted in the
art of the future. He and my grandmother Evelyn, funded the
undergraduate educations of all five of their grandchildren. Both
attended Cornell during the Depression years, and forged a will
towards lifelong frugality. My living family owes a deep debt of

gratitude to their gift, for although their hope was to secure a bright economic future for their progeny, they could not foresee the immense social and economic change that would spoil the be-Jesus out of successive generations. Still they deserve high praise for their efforts, for I believe that even if a college degree does not guarantee two cars and a garage, it can pull the individual somewhat out of ignorance in a world gone wrong. Eventually true education will pine for knowledge of the past, wherein lies the wisdom that those who cannot learn (the ignorant) or will not (the arrogant, formally educated fools), are denied. I cannot speak for my sisters and cousins, but I have been a carrier of the torch set by our ancestors. And I will (I already have) handed it over to my daughters. Henry funded Ronald's education. The DeClerq's did the same for Evelyn (college was a tool for her to find a rich husband, yet she chose Ronald, to her parent's chagrin). William and Calphurnia set up James Mott for a medical degree. Dan and Sarah Throop helped their son William become a schoolhouse teacher. No government loans. No scholarship opportunities listed on the Internet. The next generation was to have a better life, but not without hard work and responsibility. Oh yes, and up to the discovery of penicillin, most held a deep respect for a god that would take their loved ones on an insidious whim. This kept everyone's life on a less selfish, more communal trajectory. The boom economy of the mid twentieth century had the fathers working, the mothers starting to dream about work, and a new age where even their daughters could go to college to begin a career, and choose a husband who supported a wife's ambitions beyond housework and the raising of children. Wow! Progress! The kids were left home to play all day, without fieldwork and disease. Praise the home inventions and affordable access to video and vroom-vroom. Forget about those old codgers of the past. Let's party!

Well, we have lost so much in less than a century. Although I have not honored my grandparents with a choice career, at least I have gained the knowledge of whom to emulate for the next thirty summers or so.

My people.

Kurt Vonnegut wrote that there are more than enough world champions to fit into every category of human endeavor. The rest of us are poor imitators to the "great ones" of today. And we suffer a lifetime of familial loneliness for giving up the evolutionary success of clans nurtured for thousands upon thousands of years.

A western genealogy going back several generations will pin-point the dislocation for individual families. Modern technology has freed us to take a path back to a wisdom which was forgotten soon after much of the world got rich so quickly. After discovering the contents of Throops past in stored boxes I now possess the desire to shun all imitation of fools. This private education got its jump start in the public institution. For this I am grateful. It is okay to be who I am. I am so much my father and mother and the sum of all family that came before. The future is my children. The past are my ancestors. Thoreau wrote that it's "better to be a living dog than a dead lion." I disagree. The dead lions live in us all, and because of this knowledge, I rise above "dog", not by virtue of my own life necessarily, but as a result of the efforts of my forbears. They are me. I am a wonder of evolution, and my daughters will be even more suited to maneuver through life's future challenges. It is to Henry, for his reverence of the past, and to Ronald, for his steadfast hope in the future, that I dedicate this book.

Ron Throop
Oswego, N.Y.
July 4, 2012

This is not a complete genealogy. Not even close. It is to be shown in an art installation this fall which centers around por-traits painted of the direct paternal line of Throops going back to William of Barnstable Massachusetts, 1660. I know I have a mother and great mothers descending a million or so years back to equatorial Africa, and each of these human wonders had a father and mother. To think about the multitudinous lines connected in memory to just one person living today, is more the task for a math super genius than the hobbyist historian.

No, my method is for sake of congruity. I assemble the following pages with a loving touch to carry on a small portion of the work begun by my great grandfather.

So no hard feelings mothers and daughters!

If I Was Mao, Minions Would Heat Winter's Sky And Paste Leaves Back On Trees 2014. Acrylic on canvas 18 X 24"

Please Do Not Disturb For I Have Been Away On Rough Seas And Am On Leave For The Rest Of My Life 2014. Acrylic on canvas 16 X 20"

Please Do Not Disturb For I Have Been Away On Rough Seas And Am On Leave For The Rest Of My Life

It will be a private miracle if I get through the longest winter in one mental piece. I shall hang this painting up on our hotel door tonight with a $50.00 price tag. Those standard "do not disturb signs" are rude and arrogant. The hotel is a Hilton or a Hyatt so there might be some hallway passersby posing as art collectors. Maybe a hotel maid on a good tip morning. My worry is that there won't be enough room to slide the money under the door...

There it is! Caught in the act. The delusion of the artist. You can see for yourself where the thinking twists. I made the painting knowing no one will buy it, yet still plan out a procedure for selling. I have had over six months to accumulate a dowry for our daughter. Could have had plenty plus a new car if I hawked a square millimeter paint chip of Jeff Koons' mermaid hooker to my local struggling museum. But I have not made one thin dime. Monopoly money and a promissory note is tucked in her wedding card.

So this is America. The Federal Reserve, the media, the President, the Governor, the mandated lawyer and insurance agent, the top, the bottom, the middle clump, all participate in trickle down anti-poetry. To the painter unfunded, every man and woman in the street becomes the antithesis of the following verse from Lou Reed's Think it Over:

"She said somewhere there's a far away place/where all is ordered and all is grace/No one there is ever disgraced/and everybody there is wise/and everyone has taste..."

Proud Father

Our daughter gets married tomorrow. She is a whole person—loving, sensitive, self aware, joyful, and hard-working. A daughter of the traditional East born into the wild Mad Max West. Good parents of Tokyo and Bejing struggle to provide a means to achieve the like for their daughters. Education is their dowry. Bootstraps for their girls to pull up for a life of feigned equality—they are still trying to marry off the burden of daughters, but without land, the prize for the groom is a working, wage-earning partner. The misanthrope has always been a stubborn s.o.b. He locked on to his own wild west idea of child-raising as a young man put in charge of an innocent soul. Sure, learning was a huge part of it. Ironically, however, sensitivity and love were the thrust of her education. Togetherness, happiness. He worked crappy job after crappy job because he understood serious employment and pursuit of career then would hinder her immediate and long-term future well being. Overall he lost big in the money game of life. But look, look, look what has been achieved from his whole-hearted addiction to failure for a reason!

Yesterday she and her fiancé stopped over for a visit and we played cards and ate soup. She is the best thing that ever happened to me. Because of her I learned how to love, nurture, sacrifice, marry for love, and raise all future children to the best of my clown-like, cynical ability. There is a reason to be a misanthrope in life, if only to slam the door on a culture ruthlessly invading your privacy. Everyone should hate Donald Trump and despise Dick Cheney for what they are as human beings. Because of my wonderful daughter, I believe that all sensitive people (and we are a sound majority) be acutely suspicious of anyone who would respect equal rights to respiration for the Trump and Cheney monsters, and all of their descending affiliates. The latter represent what avarice in the wild west can achieve. Just ask Mr. Hilton what all the money, success and attention in the world got him for a daughter. Pure trash on the "high" hill. Become a misanthrope like me, and watch while all the scavengers scum up what garbage they can.

Thank you my beautiful child for helping me become the man I always intended to be.

Something Borrowed Something Blue 2014.
Acrylic on canvas 18 X 24"

In Santa Fe They Name Streets After Artists 2014.
Acrylic on press cleaning sheet 8 X 15"

In Santa Fe They Name Streets After Artists?

Last night is what economy does to a healthy mind and spirit. I applied to be chef at a country club. An honest job. All kinds of edible fried widgets, never in demand, but the only thing offered. This is the true economy. The interior of a new car made to look like a living room. I would want it to be more like the floor of a covered wagon but one doesn't get what one desires in economy. Coffee packaged uniformly and sold rot cheap to favor the industrialists, not the consumer. There are plenty of like-minded souls who would prefer to walk out into the groves with José and shake our own cherries off coffee bushes. No, we can only pick from what is offered. Like a job. Supply and demand is an intellectual fib crafted by robber barons and repeated by undergrads who pursued a degree in teaching because the economy refused to allow another individual entry into society. Too many of those individual rabble-rousers around and all Chinese factories would shut down. Who has ever demanded a mass produced laser copied oil painting from Target? No one. But they are there. How about a 10 ounce box of cereal for $4.29? No one. But they are still there. So much for supply and demand. More like "We supply, and you pretend to demand, or else!"

So the best our economic society can do for a lightly talented painter is place him as a line cook at a country club of pot-bellied men. Top consumers hoping to improve their handicap by day and expected to down fried oysters at night. Each one plays the game as if there could never be more than eighteen holes. Less is acceptable, but never counting in a serious way. Two or three coronary stents later they wonder, after a couple scotches (never a drink much liked, but the only one offered), why a bright guy like me is nearing 50 plating fried haddock and cobb salads to old men who would rather be served hot oatmeal and tucked into bed. "Can't say," says I, "Maybe things are better in Santa Fe, but probably nay".

Oh yes. The line cook was a lightly talented word artist too.

So to all southwestern creatives hawking their wares. Do you have room for a painter who doesn't paint like you or you? I understand how competition can be healthy for the consumer, but must be avoided by the producer at all costs. So I don't expect the wonders of Santa Fe to be revealed gratis. I just want to know if it's true that I can offer my paintings on the street. A side street. A park. Are there renegade economics professors up from Albuquerque refusing to play along with the demands of their "betters"? I mean, casual romantics, who visit Santa Fe to buy Throop art at half the cost of a Chinese factory produced Walmart original? I need to know in order to keep from doing crazy and following through with the application for kitchen manager at the local country club. For if it is true, that men and women can create their own demand for luxury goods in Santa Fe, then maybe my hometown can be cajoled into expressing their humanity by demanding that humanity be put back into our economy. Or, might I have to accept the fact that I live in a region of the country hopelessly incapable of ever building a creative economy? If the latter, then death to the spirit or a mid-life crisis move out to Santa Fe.

To put my private economic choice into words: The oily artery of a fried oyster to achieve status in Hell? Or the rice and beans of a poor painter to achieve rice and beans in Heaven?

Ill March 3 2014. Acrylic on canvas 18 X 24"

Teacher, Sorry I Painted On The Desk. I Want To Be A Ditch Digger 2014.
Acrylic on old scholar's desk

Video Games Teaching Love To Our Boys and Young Men

I guess maybe one more decade before the Pentagon meets its new quota of cannon fodder. The Iraq and Afghanistan invasions set them back a cool million or two future bodies, but the popular lust for these games should do the trick and erase all neuron connection between right and wrong.

From one critical review of Grand Theft Auto: *Playing as hardened criminals, players kill not only fellow gangsters but also police officers and innocent civilians using both weapons and vehicles while conducting premeditated crimes, including a particularly disturbing scene involving torture.*

Daddy and Mommy just want their little boy to be happy. Especially if it keeps pre-pubescent Tommy from ever becoming a sensitive, caring, and aware human being.

How brave and complete the men and women schilling graphically impressive filth on our children! Likewise, my feelings for the distinguished thugs on the Supreme Court are too warm for words. Corrupt lawyers hired for life appointments by corrupt politicians maneuvering all flora and fauna toward the goals of the mega-rich. What a fantastic system those white-wigged slavers constructed for American politics of the eighteenth and early nineteenth centuries! Men who owned men writing up a constitution that could amend itself when the future expanded beyond the six-day trip to Boston technology of the corduroy road.

Made it all the way to the Civil War and Gatling guns with only two amendments. Four score and nine years of westwardly slaughtering another race of human beings .

Then three more to "free and franchise" another race of men who were property a decade before. This also took the convincing of 600,000 poor Caucasian men rotting in mass shallow graves.

Then another fifty few years and three amendments, along with the invention of the airplane, telephone, phonograph and motion pictures, before the lucky ladies of Manland were allowed to vote, for a corrupt man of their choice of course.

Then about seven more amendments dealing mostly with the proper, gentle handling of the corrupt politicians, before passing the second to the last, giving the right to vote to 18-year old kids who were getting their legs blown off in Vietnam to protect the bad ideas and big bank accounts of the corrupt politicians.

Finally the last amendment, ratified 202 years late, which prohibits any law that increases or decreases the salary of members of the Congress from taking effect until the start of the next set of terms of office for Representatives. That's an important one, eh? 421 homicides in Chicago last year. The N.S.A. peeping in on your daughter's teenage dreams. T.S.A. gropers fondling grandmothers. Senators getting paid over ten times the poverty wage. Mountain tops eliminated for fat ugly white men in West Virginia. Video games depicting criminals as drug addict, torturing heroes.

27 Amendments. From pooping in a bowl by the fire, to the modern miracle of the Internet, the United States has continued to be the glorious constitutional republic envisioned by the Founding Fathers: corrupt, classist, and criminally insane all to the advantage of the wiggy white rich guys. Both Barack Obama and Rand Paul are wiggy white rich guys. And I don't care what Jimmy TV or Donna Ding Dong says. I follow the teachings of Martin Luther King Jr. He wouldn't let his little boy play with your filth toys made by the rich for the poor to get more stupid. Unfortunately today I think he would have to march to Mars and back to move a populace in the direction of the 28th amendment. That is, to incarcerate the entire federal government with every other Grand Theft Auto punk who gets caught.

27 amendments. What a phony baloney constitution!

Sorry I Didn't Make It Down To Boca. I Got Hung Up In Oswego 2014.
Acrylic on canvas 24 X 18"

Friday Night Out With Adjunct Art Professor 2014.
Acrylic on canvas 24 X 18"

Friday Night Out With Adjunct Art Professor

Higher education in the arts. An oxymoron, but only because I am educated and think I know what that word means. So, English adjuncts too, they also sit across from me like the man in the painting struggling with private demons day after day.

I have much to write on this subject, but I will try my best to keep it short and personal. Brevity is the new black. Our Internet God gets suspicious of words after they fill up a whole page without selling anything. So here goes...

Number one: Any provost of a college or university who partakes in the adjunct system of hiring experts at a pittance needs a light tar and heavy feathering. This gang mentality of tenure-track professorship vs. under-insured low-pay adjunct teaching is a paradigm replete with local collegiate classism. In a word it is *disgusting.* In a phrase—*vile, petty, and incomprehensibly unfair weasel games.* A nearby college where a friend of mine teaches will not afford him a private office on the hill. A room must be shared by all the lowly "unmade" adjuncts. Of course among the hapless professors in that room there may be a great teacher worthy of a private phone line, if not a club-issued award. The majority of students might sign up for his class because he is knowledgeable, enthusiastic, and talented beyond his rank in the art of pedagogy. But the provost and her good ole girls/boys club does not inquire about actual teaching experience or ability when interviewing for the private office. The credentials can be equal, but one of those lucky 40 or 50 applicants gets the prize of being able to support a family and leave his day-old travel mug on the desk. The rest painstakingly struggle with a used car payment and harbor serious reservations about extra sprinkles on their kid's ice cream cones.

It just makes for a vile, petty, unfair, even childish system of higher education. It puts fear into all players, nourishes elitism, bullyism, gives men and women of the same age and caliber a false measuring stick to guide their lives by. It fosters competition toward the wrong ends (status and avarice), and of course the student body suffers. Heck, the latter have no idea about the immense gulf in pay, benefits and respect between the made and the unmade. They assume (their parents too) that the enormous sums spent on tuition is equally divided among the campus faculty, with slight variations in senior and junior pay. In fact, knowing the truth about below poverty income for their kid's mentors, might make a significant number of parents rethink their plan to invest money in a school that is practically starving its local intelligentsia.

So no more multimillion dollar buildings please, while good people are getting paid bad wages. Don't believe administration, my adjunct professor friends, when it declares that your pay is equivalent to a dishwasher's salary because the money for the big building comes from a special fund allotted to construction projects. They are lying to you. Their line is called "management confidential". Confidential means "lie" on a college level entrance exam. Don't let them lie to you anymore. Tell your students what you get paid, and what Ms. Cheese, the senior professor, gets paid. Show the gap to close the gap. Ms. Cheese teaches like a wet cardboard box. Some of you, I am sure articulate more meaning-fully on relevant subjects than Ms. Cheese could with the help of a marching band. The kids don't need to know what past credentials their teacher has layered thick upon her super smart sandwich. They want public and self respect, knowledge, and the ability to prove what they are capable of. Similar to the needs of an adjunct professor struggling to make ends meet on a line weighted down by corrupt multimillion dollar colleges and universities.

Number two: The previous painting is in reference to art faculty working everyday to silence their own art. What a conflict of inter-est! The more immersed and dependent on the university one is, the less his creativity can explore. The art teacher must be careful of how he is regarded among peers and powerful administrators. The problem builds over time to complete an endless vicious circle. Careful teachers teaching careful art to students to become careful teachers themselves one day. Institutional art. In a hyphenated word, anti-art.

Recently the Agora Gallery, a well-respected vanity show place in New York, linked an article for its Twitter followers. It was about the possible culture boom wrought by the fracking gush in North Dakota. The Agora hires people who have art degrees. Art in North Dakota. An oxymoron like "mountain man of the Bowery". Men and women well drillers out to make some damn good art. They come home with twisted spines and chemical lung, and rush through dinner to express their dreams with pen or paint. I see it now, culture in North Dakota, like gay Paris. Painters in three-egg diners guzzling vanadium water instead of absinthe. Children being taught by well drillers who have aspired to art. Young adults graduating from the University of North Dakota with art degrees interviewed to adjunct at my local college. "Are you kidding us? We can get paid ten times that licking boots at the Marcellus Shale fields. Up yours with this insult to my climb out of poverty."

So to art professors I say,

Good for art, bad for oyster-fed artists, but truly, all art teachers must be made adjuncts, and live on rice and beans, and sometimes beer, or else!

That, for the artists. The rest of university adjuncts need to mob up, and storm the Bastille of administration to publicly shame the politicos who dangle their careers on a string.

Google Maps Provides A Masochistic Soirée To Poor Girls Seeking Sea Air
2014. Acrylic on canvas 16 X 20"

Google Maps Provides a Masochistic Soirée To Poor Working Girls Seeking Sea Air

I am seeking sponsorship by a very rich person, famous or not. I am willing to give up a third of my collection for $5,465.00. I need to take my wife on a Pacific Coast Highway trip to inspire in her a near future move out of this cold, condemning Hell of upstate New York. I have a lot of paintings. This will be a good investment, for I am told by my minor gossip mother that my minor millionaire uncle just spent the same sum on window treatments for a couple rooms in his downstairs living area. Now, I haven't seen these window treatments, but I am sure they are uplifting. Every time he walks by them he must see my aunt in a new light, making her skin smoother, her step easier, and his lustful advances feel almost semi-successful. It is the power of a well rendered window treatment, as any minor millionaire in America knows, to take old lovers on a stroll down memory lane and inspire them to court life and loving once again. Not that my paintings can compare to drapery stitched by unhappy maidens in the Philippines, or wood blinds hand crafted in a Brazilian sweatshop. Yet unlike glorious window treatments, automobiles that rust, and relationships fed on money and not enthusiasm, a third of my present archive will not depreciate. And, as added bonus, one can have revolving decoration throughout the home for a lifetime. The truth is, anyone rich enough to spend nearly six grand on my paintings, most likely can afford the window treatments too. So nothing lost and much gained.

Millionaires and thousandaires too... Let's invest in Throop work now to complement your drapery. I see Rose and I riding free and easy down the Pacific Coast Highway on a bright blue May morning. I have worked all year in my glum studio singing praises of love, laughter, and romance. I tell you sometimes it took what amounted to pulling rusty shrapnel out of my soft tissue to achieve those praises, but I managed, every time. Rose has a riding scarf on, and sunglasses. I look how Kurt Vonnegut must have felt the day he got his first royalty check for writing misanthropic literature. Proud.

We stop in Monterey and I hawk my unframed paintings along

the roadside of Veteran's Park. A lady with a dog buys one. That means for once, I got lunch covered. After the second glass of wine, Rose agrees to a move out west. "We'll do it," she says. "God Ron, you just sold one of your paintings in the street!"

"I know. And she said she'll hang it prominently as soon as the interior decorators are finished sizing her blinds."

We drive down the road and lay up for the night in the parking lot of Nepenthe Restaurant, after a warm slow sway on the bar's dance floor. Tomorrow we will hike down the path to pay homage to Henry Miller, say a prayer for the millionaire lady walking her dog, praise the Gold Rush for stealing California, and then fall asleep on a cliff edge dreaming eternity.

All that from Google Maps. Hot damn the American Window Treatment!

My Heart's Desire Is That One Of You Is Drunk Enough To Buy This Painting 2014. Acrylic on canvas, 17 X 17"

Is There Just One Gold-Digger Left In Naples Empathetic To Barely Talented Painters? 2014. Acrylic on canvas 18 X 24"

Is There One Gold-digger Left In Naples Empathetic To Barely Talented Painters?

Here is a desperate shark, beached off the waters of the Gulf Coast. He is nonplussed by the fact that no matter how many times he fin hops out onto the sand, the gold digging humans just pretend to look the other way. Not one sardine for his humiliating dance. No flaky tuna. Not even a saucy anchovy scraped off a pizza pie. Sometimes he goes back to sea at night wondering if his failure is in the delivery. Should he wear clown make-up? A flower hat? Hire a sea anemone sidekick with a nihilistic sense of humor? What is the scam, he wonders while swimming to the depths, that will keep his head just below water? "There is always tomorrow," his wife assures him. "Hang out here with me and the other sharks by the spa pipe sticking out of the sea floor. There's a black ooze that Thelma swears by. It will smooth out your sand paper skin. You should stop painting. The humans want nothing to do with the perspective of an expressive shark".

Tomorrow is always a new day. Eventually he will give up the song and dance. The black ooze is so comforting. Anyway, all that was ever asked of him was to be a shark, scent fear and blood, and participate in specie groupthink. No different from human being really.

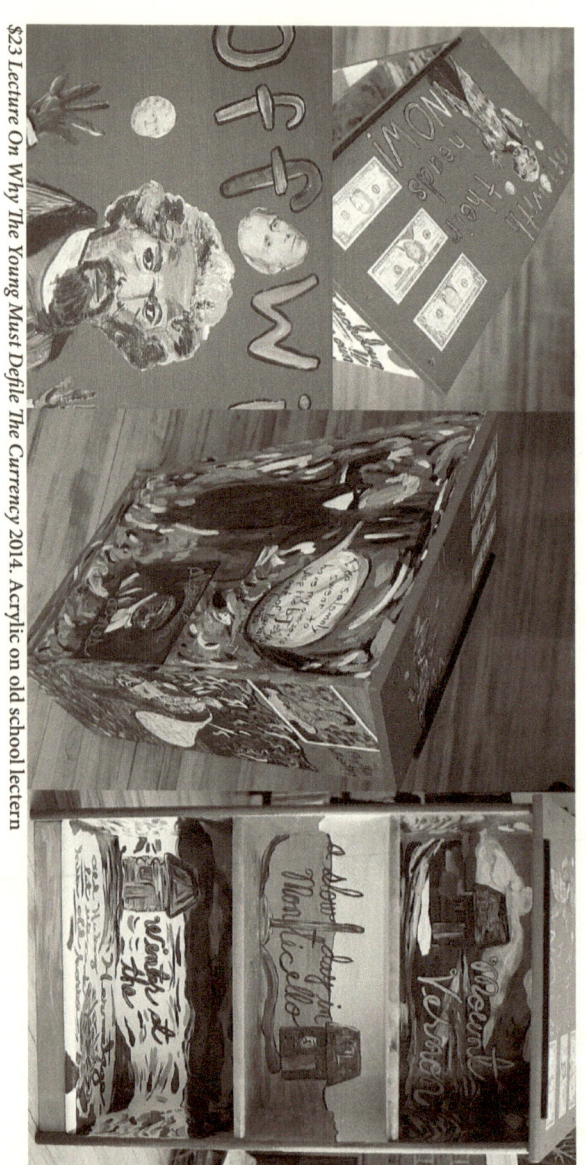

$23 Lecture On Why The Young Must Defile The Currency 2014. Acrylic on old school lectern

$23 Lecture On Why The Young Must Defile The Currency

Justice can be found by taking cerebral baby steps. It's never far from the truth, which any child or enlightened adult can reveal quickly if confronted by a wrong. Law, on the other hand, is determined by a toddler with mouth sewn shut, glued to a Rube Goldberg ball, and sent rolling from the better part of a day (a minor traffic ticket) to upwards of oblivion or longer (premeditated revenge killing). The tremendous apparatus of law was constructed by the children of wealthy planters and industrialists who raised an outlaw nation on the strong backs of recently descended Africans and dirt poor Ellis Island immigrants. Law made slavery, the Civil War, tenement houses, and 400 homicides in Chicago last year. Today the government snubs its free citizens with constant monetary reminder of oppression's dark past. Law works 'round the clock for the owners of a society, both antebellum and modern. Yesterday the planter class. Today the banker class, skeevy private plane persons who are probably not too far removed ancestrally from the planter class. Hence, slave owners in our wallets. People who owned/own people. Presidents who owned less people before becoming President, and then got to be head of state, and bought more people to make themselves richer. They were dirty privies. Yesterday and today.

Many established university historians make the argument that these men were products of their time, as if every one born American had a 3/5 person to call their own. White women, men without property, and all little farmer girls and boys not of Africa were burdened by the same good fortune wrought by a slaver economy. No. Not even close. A majority of dark people were owned by a small "planter" class of Caucasian men, who needed a culture of racism and prejudice to reap their private goodies.

Yet no matter how crisp and clear my hindsight, arguments above do not justify pasting these "men of their time" on today's currency. We have a diverse freer nation now. The land is ours, inherited by revolutionary thieves, who themselves inherited it from metal working colonial squatters. So why are these thieves still "owning" our coinage? Have no other good men and women been born after their usurpation? Why people anyway? How about the

woodchuck, turkey, pickerel, or pike? How about a purple mountain majesty, a geyser, a Great Lakes chain? Canada trades a loon
and an English Queen. Freakish. But at least no slaveholders.

So, to the preceding piece. Three presidents who owned (and got
rich) off slaves. I painted a lectern because I think all good Americans need revisited history lessons. I took a $1, $20, and $2 bill and
glued them to the top. I carefully cut out the heads on each and
lobbed them over to Frederick Douglas to juggle. I replaced the cut
out holes with heads of decent and good people from revolutionary America. Phillis Wheatley where Washington was. Absalom
Jones in place of Jackson. Finally, Benjamin Banneker to replace
Jefferson on the forgotten, yet still circulating two dollar bill. I
also invisible-inked the money with a fact about the slave holding
history of each. A black light reveals the truth. For instance on the
twenty dollar bill one who possesses the necessary equipment will
read the following: "Jackson was paternal with his slaves although
I do not think he fathered any."

On the left side of the lectern is Washington holding the true
meaning of the Declaration of Independence. Phillis Wheatley was
a poet who did not general the death of anyone nor own another
human being. Leave it to the hyperactive painter to misspell her
name. Sorry *Phillis*.

On the right side is Jefferson, excited in the prospect of ravaging
young girls. He will father a child with one of his slaves. Kind of
like the guy in Cleveland who stole three girls off the street and
locked them in his basement for ten years. Benjamin Banneker
was not known to be a serial pervert, and he authored a beautiful
almanac.

On the front is Andrew Jackson, the most vile, with his face
burning off in Hell. Absalom Jones was a clergyman who tended to
plague victims during the Yellow Fever epidemic in Philadelphia
in 1794. Coincidentally, George Washington, featured on another
panel of cowardice, hightailed it out of the infected city and didn't
come back until all the bugs were dead.

There are three shelves in the lectern, each depicting slave quar-
ters at the estates of the currency Presidents.

They read respectively:

Mount Vernon B&B—Sleeps 18

A slow day in Monticello (notice the empty whipping post)

Winter at the Hermitage—Old Hickory let us cook his old horse

I plan to show the lectern at my local art association. I will invite the history and economics departments from our state college, and local school districts. There is so much our children can learn from our money. They never asked for the hero-making of lessor men. Why do we give them these dead racist kings? I wish to see a just currency replacement before my grandchild's first lemonade stand. These Presidents are historical. Each has an importance to history. But they were not good men. Intelligent? Yes. Crafty? You betcha. So was Adolf Hitler. I forget now... Which euro honors his triumphant legacy?

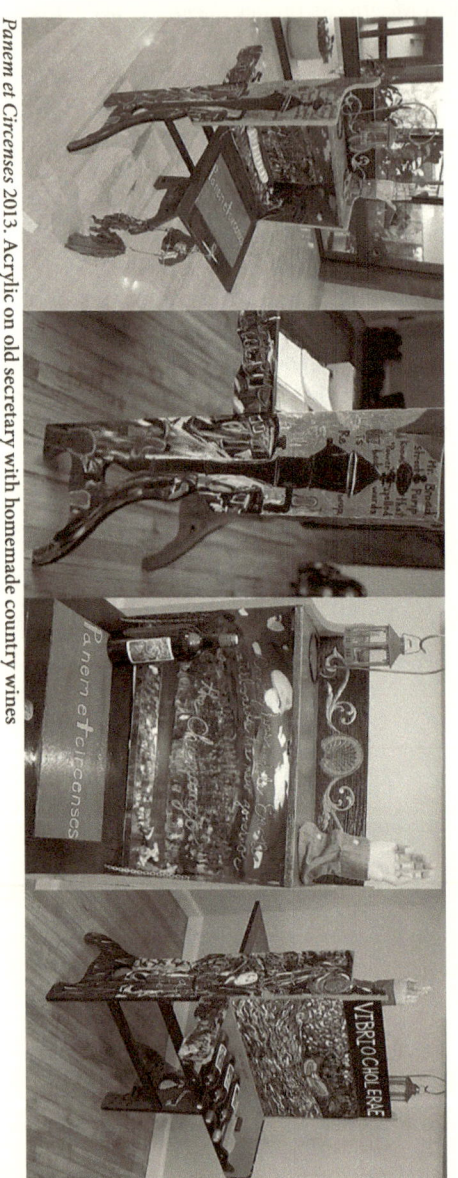

Panem et Circenses 2013. Acrylic on old secretary with homemade country wines

Panem et Circenses

The "Bread and Circuses" wine bar. 2013. An old secretary turned into a morality kiosk to display my politics and country wines. New York summers are a fruity lush paradise. The forager can feel all squire-like berry picking along the public road. With some vine yeast and modest initial investment in equipment, delicious, potent wines can be had by the time the five month lock down of a New York winter temporarily close all doors to hope, health and happiness.

Elderberry, dandelion, blueberry, and my personal favorite, blackberry. They are high proof, delusion of grandeur wines, aged just long enough to make the common man feel as powerful as any Governor* coached in the backseat of a black SUV.

First off, please note that it is an opinion piece. I am one of those rare modern fools who still preserves some quirky 19th century, human morals. Especially in matters of life and death. Winter, by virtue of the wine, recharge my dreams of equality, and I convince myself that, beyond communal law, no person has authority over another. That is, the Golden Rule should be the only indicator applied to all community problems—local, state, national, private, and public. Of course no democratic or totalitarian regimes ever abide by this simple application of human justice. And anarchism, which is likely impossible, is a label word reserved for the young and dumb, who might actually believe that such a system applied would preserve texting and orange juice for lunch when desired. On the other hand, localism is a word to scare the designer underwear off any crooked piece of garbage humanoid, who would suffer most under its auspices. That is, representatives of the multimillion billion dollar corporations—puppets easily placed into positions of power and influence. Our present day Governor* being one such corporito empowered by a system at war with the Golden Rule.

I sincerely believe in the libertarian idea of nullification, but only if backed up by a local economy. There are 19 million people living in this state. One Governor* and two parties, made up of many corrupt lawyers do not represent even the tiniest fraction of our families. They support ideas, loud ones, that seldom come from the hearts and minds of the real men and women who vote in November. Manufactured debates, wedge issues, to line up one candidate against the other, when both are just nefarious Party stooges snorting coke at private functions.

Which leads to one panel of the secretary with the following text: *The Farmer-governor Teaches the Coke-sniffing Governor* Empathy on a Stick. My ancestor Enos Throop was Governor of New York State from 1829-1832. He was not re-elected because he was a farmer in a time when a farmer had to answer to each one of his farmer neighbors. His farmer neighbors did not want the Governor to tax them so that the farmers of Hamilton, Binghamton and Utica could have the state build a canal (the Chenango) to enrich their farms. Hence the interior of the secretary where I have Enos water board our present day Governor*. Why not? The President* declares that his minions at the CIA* have that right. So my imagination can too.

Another panel depicts the water-born disease of cholera, so often epidemic in 19th century America. Enos had to deal with the outbreak during his governorship, through no fault of his own. He traveled to inflicted towns and cities to oversee the tragedy and spread the idea of calm leadership throughout the panic. Cholera ruled the streets before Mr. Snow put the new science into practice, locally, without multimillion dollar profit driven research by GlaxoSmithKline*. The dandy choleras are out enjoying a Sunday evening stroll past the Broad Street pump.

On the back is a rack for the country wines, and a homage to the famous old west U.S. Marshal entitled *Leadership During the Time of the Cholera.*

Individual homemade country wines bear the following labels:

Dandelion toluene/a glass of golden sea/a cheap, if less efficient/ lobotomy

Blackberry—Ready or Not/V2O5/Try to keep your kids alive

Blueberry—Share this with a lover to woo/or a close friend to confide/ C5H8O2/or just glutaraldehyde

Elderberry Heaven/Elderberry Hell/offer Mr. Cuomo/ a glass of HCL

Finally the secretary's legs are dressed up with a skeletal Cuomo gesticulating with the words: "Andrew doth dance 'round the leukemic hole Jole".

And the Devil with, "Satan cries a toluene tear".

There is a human hand holding a salt loaf of bread, dried basil and tobacco strung around a piece of shale with a photograph of Cuomo and a painting of Throop pasted on a rock. I displayed the wine bar last spring and summer with an essay handout authored by yours truly, and an old speech by Governor Throop (that he wrote himself), explaining his position on the future construction of the Chenango Canal. Both are written by men bearing a conscience. A virtue that power brokers in the present day state of New York fear like rational people fear a family-shrinking infected water supply.

Come to the wine bar and we shall toast the nullification of corrupt human beings, which today means anyone seeking power as a representative in New York State.

If I Was Mao The Super Bowl Would Be Full of Milk and Propagandists

Last night was this year's foray into the wonderful world of modern media insanity. The off-the-gridders who still abide by life-saving advances in modern science and medicine, provided they interact with at least two other like-minded families within walking distance, might have answers for youth seeking wisdom. Because it sure ain't coming from Chrysler's new stooge Bob Dylan, or Rupert Murdock's Midas pedophile look-alike touch. If I were Mao, both of these sorry old men would be treading milk in my super bowl, along with every other celebrity name I didn't know last night (but unfortunately do now). All of them proof that money and fame are just two dead leaves swirling in gigundo voids of their own private Hells. We, the fathers and mothers, owe our children deep, profound apology for allowing these perverted millionaires and billionaires access in to their hopeful hearts and minds. Maybe, if truly humble, a head bowed down forever in shame of a today that will not move an immovable mountain to improve the luck of a crap shoot tomorrow.

Clean corporate filth reminding us to be jingoistic, love the NFL, and buy another two ton rolling box of loneliness that rusts. Bob Dylan ain't no born again Christian. I hear you have to believe in Hell to be one of those. Bruce Willis? Another die hard loser. And Paul Allen, the glorious owner of the Seattle Seahawks? A slave-holder. Graciously showering the stadium in milk on a Sunday, when the lot of us are lactose intolerant.

John Lennon explained it to us easily in a few verses. But he never got the chance to grow to be a man, and provide to his young boys a possible solution. I think that if he survived fame and a gunshot wound, there might have been a wise old celebrity born from that angst. His commercial would try to end a war by making war on the propagandists. He'd go broke trying while the rest of us got old thinking about fresh carpet smells in new cars and Scarlett Johansson cleavage that we will never ever touch.

*If I Were Mao, The Super Bowl Would Be Full Of Milk
And Propagandists* 2014. Acrylic on canvas 24 X 18"

Mortality Smortality 2014. Acrylic on panel board 64 X 48"

Paul's Big M In Oswego, N.Y.

A hot, lazy Sunday and I was off to buy some parmesan cheese
for the pasta and the Bolognese. Paul's Big M is now the only store
in town that sells it grated in cups and weighed. But to get it, I am
forced to run the gauntlet of human misery and woe. The aisles are
thin, one needs to either wait or ask politely to pass another shop-
per. So I get a good, close look at Paul's patrons. One in a hundred
might appear to have witnessed satori at some point in adult life,
but the other 99 walk and talk like Hell is time on earth and Jesus
won't take them after Paul's Big M no matter what. I have been
coming here reluctantly for 25 years yet I have never met Paul.
Maybe he's a man like me who has become mentally ill from his
time in Oswego and because he can afford it, sequesters himself in
a corner office rather than mingle with Hell's flightless angels.

It is that bad. New Agers would argue that it is my self, project-
ing unhappiness on to the miserable faces of Paul's clientele, but
these days New Agers write and wonder from metropolises, where
any delusional hopeful can find affirmative philosophies simply
using the law of averages. For instance, every downtrodden ignorant misfit in San Francisco can be countered with twelve New
Agers lying to themselves with a paycheck. The trends keep chang-
ing and reappearing because life is always good, and everyone is
happy or it's their own damn fault because they didn't pick the
right major in college. San Francisco is now in the habit of making
toast chic. Give me geographical and economic power over the
most positive Zen faker in San Francisco for just six months, and
I will make her boil with bitterness after a brief Oswego residency.
She will beg for airfare back to the mega-lie faster than you can say
Oswego County Opportunities. All the books published. All those
informative, intelligent interviews on NPR! The metropolis lying
to itself so grandly, so feverishly, while begging the live long day
to get noticed. "Get a hold of some fine Italian parmesan cheese,"
instructs *The Splendid Table* radio show host. She says "parmesan" like no self-respecting Italian ever would. She says it like any
middle management American urbanite wants to hear it, else take
a dive off the Golden Gate Bridge. I listen to her show on the way

back home with my plastic cup of fine Wisconsin parmesan. Some nefarious twang in her voice, like she would secretly euthanize my whole miserable community if it were prerequisite to reaching a wider audience.

She and NPR are elitist only if one believes that higher beings reside outside themselves. I do not. Everyman in post-industrial America is what one of us is here at Paul's Big M in Oswego, N.Y. Each smiling, scowling, or indifferent face is representative of us all. I am an elitist. Yet I would suffer my fellow shopping mortals no different fate from my own. I do not want their private joys to suffer. I just want them to end. When I say "excuse me" or "pardon me sir", I expect eye contact and a reply. Otherwise their lives must disappear. I would expect the same philosophy from their point of views. I do not want the chance to live among men if I cannot elevate my respect for others even if it is phony. We all hit the pillow at night thinking over our private joy and dread. None of us needs a circus mirror to exacerbate our problems. So the tattooed meth addict pulling off his shirt outside of a Paul's Big M needs to disappear as he yells into his cell phone "I don't know what the fuck her problem is" while a five-year-old girl holding hands with her grandfather approaches the electric door thinking fairies. His joy need not suffer. He just needs to disappear.

Misanthropy is not a very effective social philosophy. I wonder if it's even fair at all. I cannot just hate human beings. It doesn't make sense. Raccoons don't hate other raccoons. They compete, which is healthy, entrepreneurial. It makes for building a better raccoon character and hence, society. But humans don't work like that. We all hate and fear each other. Why? Maybe because we expect some level playing field, such as the raccoon's, but are denied it. Say a world where there is a likelihood of death by starvation, so a Payless and JC Penny are out of the question. After religious morals are discounted there is no more marker for being human. We have no idea anymore what it means to be of mankind like a raccoon is so obviously a raccoon. It is either good or bad, or somewhere in between of the sameness all raccoons share and understand. The father ate his baby raccoon or he didn't, but among other raccoons, no judgment was made. Human fathers aren't supposed to kill their babies or other people's babies. Supposedly that is a part of being human. Still, many, many do—serial killers, passion murderers, aggressive pedophiles, sociopaths, soldiers and governments. It's not so easy with humans. So there exists an irony with the whole human concept. It seems that we exist by the philosophy that one can live and let live until somebody loses too much blood out of a bullet hole. See? Doesn't make sense. Only the mentally ill would argue against the Golden Rule, but rarely is it ever followed, from the innocence of a white lie to the violent trespass of armed robbery. And yet we all claim to be human.

Maybe this irony would exist for raccoons too if they "evolved", (a euphemism describing the eventual advent of the A-bomb), into Internet shoppers and consumers of automobiles bearing delusional names like "Highlander" and "Avenger". Maybe.

Without a judgmental king or trusted God, modern, wealthy societies have no fear marker to guide them. No indelible code of conduct. Today our children are abandoned to the concept of making it up as they go. Acceptance of societal degeneration is the parental new black. And of course if the rabbi, minister, tribal chief, or imam are not controlling the media, then we get more live and let live lost souls reporting on what is right and wrong. Doomed to failure. Exponential failure with few ideas for change.

Well, I have one.

I believe our society could be saved with uniforms. A code strictly enforced from birth until death, every man and woman must abide by wearing the same exact uniform, fit to size of course. Every other aspect of life in America can remain the same. Paul's Big M can stock the same chalky, processed foods. Ford can make cars in Mexican factories, and drones can spy on our babies' pee parts in their bath water. Eagle and Chinese calligraphy tattoos may flourish but no one will see them unless they're drawn on face, hands, and feet since the uniform is pant length and long-sleeved. Every man and woman the same visually, so the heart, good or bad, can be judged without distraction. The thug with the mouth oblivious to the little girl and her grandfather can still act crudely, but maybe now the offended will speak up, or perhaps grandpa might find the social stamina to whack the thug on the shin with an iron pipe. The latter will be wise to retreat seeing all the concerned uniformed people stopping to assess the scene. Dressed like every one else, he no longer inspires that initial fear-jerk that aggressively dressed assholes were once able to muster. He looks just like neighbor Fred mowing his lawn. And neighbor Fred is always aware when children are around.

Gangs in Chicago stop ganging. The Homicide Boys won't be able to tell an Imperial Gangster from a Nike Boy. Bor-ing. Can't tell if the innocent bystander is a degenerate or a mailman. And people always just laugh at any attempt of a silly gangster strut on the street.

The military will become more democratic. If private Tom looks like General Bob it will be extremely difficult for Bob to convince Tom to run up front where the bullets are hissing.

The Republic is saved. Everybody is on the level. When a senatorial candidate arrives to the rally in a chauffeured SUV, the constituents laugh, laugh, laugh, knowing he will never possess a character brighter than his uniform. Everyone will want to vote for the chauffeur. Humility will become Gandhi-popular as never before.

The economy will constrict to the point of personal salvation. People will want to become self-determinate once again. New declarations of independence will arise. "Jesus, I look just like this ignorant jackass beside me in the grocery aisle. Get me some land and a hoe, and children to instruct on the miracles of love and knowledge. I don't want to be a 'regular guy,' or 'just one of the folks'."

These days there are just too many arbitrary visual markers predicting individual character.

If we must abide by the philosophy to live and let live (knowing that very few ever do), then let us raise that contradiction to a level playing field. Uniforms I say. At the very least, they will make for more pleasant shopping in all wasted and spent towns and cities like Oswego, Amerika.

Find Love Close Hell—O Nurse 2014. Acrylic on canxas 18 X 24"

Queen Nutella® Shines The Herkimer Diamond 2014. Acrylic on canvas 36 X 48"

Shame As A Future Necessity For Society

The newspapers have published the value of Lou Reed's estate, two-thirds of which was amassed post mortem, because financially, a poet is worth more dead than alive, period. At the time of death it totaled 10 million, but now is up to 30 million and rising in value every day.

In my opinion 10 million dollars was no great sum for one of the greatest poet-musicians to ever have struggled on planet earth. One whose work was also distributed world-wide, and potentially revered by anyone who has ever loved.

That is saying a lot. And it is true. He worked. He gave. He lived and left a modest estate compared to others of equal stature on the world stage who strutted publicly in order to make a living.

My grandfather was a state engineer who, by thrift, left an estate equivalent to what 10 million would buy today. Enough to put five grandchildren through private colleges and universities, and provide a life without financial worry for my grandmother. So Lou left a frugal engineer's legacy, when he could have sold out like any corporation puppy dog—like the Bob Dylan hiding inside each one of us creative feelers, who jones for the opportunity to make a killing if ever the chance arrives.

Lou wrote and gave melody to this:

"She said 'Somewhere there's a far away place
Where all is ordered and all is grace
No one there is ever disgraced
And everybody there is wise
And everyone has taste.'"

Hope and conscience poetry. In his will he left a percentage to his wife and sister, the latter to use the money to take care of their ailing mother.

This is all very good news to me. Creative careers matter; disproportionally low financially, compared to more secure professions, yet on a potential money level, equal to what the upper middle class would be able to amass carefully over time. Successful accountants, lawyers, even speculating land men could leave an estate equal to Lou's if careful with investments over the years. A couple I know by association, the Millers, who I use often in my writing to juxtapose the crap shoot of capitalism in America, have already reached Lou's legacy and beyond at just middle age. I compare their surface life story to Lou's to illustrate the turning point in evolution of our species.

I had a puppy crush on the wife Barbara Miller when she was a young girl. Beyond that, I know nothing more than what her mother has shared with my mother who tells the Miller's stories to me from time to time. She enjoys their shock-entertainment value. I use them as anecdotal evidence of why I believe society needs to reinvigorate shame as an effective deterrent to our descent into chaos and a new living hell that awaits.

Barbara works light. She is the president of a local bakery corporation her husband purchased to spare her from a life of boredom. Larry Miller is a trained lawyer who buys property very low and uses his influence to receive local and state government help, whether it be to build a new road via eminent domain through a farmer's working hundred year old apple orchard, or twenty years of tax breaks offered to the strip mall franchises leasing Larry's properties. He brought his town the best Walmarts and Gander Mountains money can buy, and in a dwindling economy, helped turn his struggling neighbors into a subsistent army of minimum wage soldiers. Financial success has come to the Millers. Already world travelers and proud owners of three homes, one in Florida where their gardeners trim Rose bushes next door to Jon BonJovi's hired men. Neither Barbara nor Larry cook or clean, and their children are going to good colleges.

Their assets, I surmise, were about equal to Lou Reed's at the poet's time of death.

That is where their comparison ends—at the means to an end. And here is where I hand out rotten fruit to my countrymen still capable of discriminating between a life living the confusion of love and one that worships wealth.

What type of personality truly loves a strip mall? Who drives down a car-congested boulevard overflowing with personal well-being on his way to pick up soap and camping gear? All of us partake in the present economy. Rich or poor. Even Barbara finds fantastic deals at Kohl's or Target from time to time. Her husband has provided the community with easy shopping, often leading to or exacerbating bad taste, normalizing consumerism, and ever widening the gap between adulthood and fulfillment. He enriches himself via a routine that is of the lowest level. He is winning the culture war because each of us (including both Larry and Barbara) are mentally deranged to a degree.

Well distributed poets such as Lou Reed, heal from time to time, when hearts are open and aloneness is welcome. Clear Channel knows this. That is why poetry is not sung over the airwaves. It is anti-business. Getting drunk and screwed is okay, just don't be prepared to think with a conscience. So Lou's lyrics and melodies sneak through because during a weak moment as a young man, he wrote and recorded "Take a Walk on the Wild Side," and Candy was giving head, so all the young people begging for content began to think their local DJ was rad, when it was really an established media choice made by the top dogs at headquarters to include Lou on their drinking and screwing party play list. So Lou got "cool" overnight and abandoned to obscurity even quicker because he chose to pursue his inner genius rather than promote meaning-lessness for a lifetime. He made more than enough money preach-ing poetry backed by melody. And he did it without licking boots, a near miracle in this time of celebrity worship.

Our family made a trip yesterday to Barne's and Noble, another Larry Miller strip mall creation. A necessary evil to book browse for our daughter's summer reading suggestions. As always, I made a bee-line to educational materials, Rose to graphic design, and our daughter straight to the shelves stocking the latest manga. Op-posite my aisle was a table stacked with books. The sign on it read, Books that make you think. On it were works having nothing in common besides the fact that reading them might exercise our brains, and also seek the counsel of our consciences. Vonnegut's *Slaughterhouse Five* beside Harper Lee's *To Kill a Mockingbird*. One anti-war, the other anti-segregation. Both displaying the very ugly side of humanity. Books with a moral philosophy to uphold, harboring meaningful content, piled high on a reserved table. Some corporate upstart with a fresh idea. "Books to make 'em think, Charlie, or at least pretend to think while nursin' a choco-late coffee in our Internet café."

What kind of author ever penned a novel or the like with the intention not to make people think? Initially, even Stephen King and John Grisham set out, I'm sure, to receive thoughtful response from their readers. Of course they failed, and in that failure found fame and fortune. No irony with a *Time to Kill* spotted in the back seat of a Prius parked at a Red Lobster. None at all. It is exactly what should be expected from a John or Jane Doe who allow a Larry and Barbara Miller to build upon wealth and status initially realized by failure of conscience. They believe it awaits them too, as long as John and Jane continue to seek purchasing solace along the strip mall of Anytown, America. *Slaughterhouse Five* spotted in the car at an Outback, however, is not only ironic, but very dangerous to the future comfort of a Larry and Barbara Miller. Two cars a conspiracy, and needing only three aiding and abetting Vonnegut at the same Outback to make a declaration of revolution, a strip mall stripped of all Chinese do-dads, and the Millers shamed out loud at all future public appearances.

To my logic, consumerism cannot be a healthy mutation for our species. From the standpoint of evolution, it might suggest an imminent leveling off, a massive culling to a point of near extinction. High greed and low greed are still greed, which in itself is anti-growth. My obvious reverence for the artist Lou Reed does not elevate him morally to a position much higher than the Millers. He just made a wiser career choice because he left something good of himself that was so much more than charity wrought from guilt, which is the only good the Miller's will ever be able to pass on. Lou Reed created thought through poetry and shared it with music. Sure there was the rough stuff—broken backs and used vials washed up on the beach. But his work is also pregnant with love, justice and morality. He left the like of strip mall parking lots full of used cars each stuffed to the torned-fabric ceiling with shaming ammunition. It was worth 10 million dollars to him. Now it is humanity's responsibility to use it.

Larry and Barbara Miller should be shamed, but Americans are just too darn polite. I quote the entirety of "Tripitena's Speech" from Lou's 2003 release *The Raven* to get the ball rolling for tomorrow's morality revolution. It will either come dressed dandy American or brutally ugly like Mao. Best to begin training our minds now for the changes to come. Synapse pathways need to realign.

"Tripitena's Speech" by Lou Reed

My love
The king by any other name a pissoir
You, my love tower over them all
They are but vermin beneath your heels
They are monkeys
Suit them, frame them to your own vision
But do not let one false word
Of mockery seep through to your vast heart
I have seen you from close and afar and your worth
Far exceeds your height, your width
The depth of your sorrow
Oh willful outcast doth thou not see the light of our love
Our linked fortunes
Our hearts melded together
Into one fine golden braided finery

They listen to the music of idiots and amuse themselves
With the sordid Miseries of their businesses
They are not the things of angels
Nor of any higher outpost that humanity might aspire to
Your loathsome vomitous
Businessman king is of the lowest order
His advisors
Crumbling mockeries of education driven by avarice
My love
Dress them in the suits of mockery
And in their advanced state of stupidity
And senility
Burn and destroy them so their ashes might join the compost
Which they so much deserve
If justice on this earth be fleeting
Let us for once hear the weeping
And the braying of the businessman king
Let them be the orangutans they are
And set them blazing from the chandelier for all to see
Hanging from the ceiling by their ridiculous chains
And petticoats which you will have them wear
Under the guise of costumic buffoonery
He who underestimates
In time is bound to find the truth sublime
And hollow lie upon the grates of systemic disorder
Businessmen

You're not worth shitting on

The First Iron Night Of August 2014. Acrylic on birch panel 48 X 24"

Joy—It's What's In The Head

Marie and I celebrated our crystal anniversary on Thursday and I was able to carry the weight of good feeling into the weekend. Just barely.

Five years ago we bought land in the country for the price many Americans would pay for a Toyota 4Runner. 16 acres surrounded at three cardinal directions by 1400 acres of the county nature center. Just a few humans every couple of square miles. The cool cloudy day of our anniversary was good medicine. Marie suggested that I paint her, which I did on a piece of 2 x 4' luan. It will be hidden in the basement until our teenage daughter is not that grossed out by it—probably forever. I drank expensive local craft beer followed by local Finger Lakes Red Wine (dry like my humor, thank Dionysus). We picked blackberries, cooked dinner over the fire, and went for a rare bugless walk at dusk, to finally fall asleep with sunset still marking the tree line.

We can't afford the land anymore. It's paid for, but our debts in other places not nearly as valuable, are bearing down on us. The "for sale" sign has been up for several months without any takers. Lucky for us, for we're getting cold feet—especially after a crystal anniversary cementing silver and golden ones to come so long as our bodies can hold out that long. I am a stubborn creative fool hiding in happy failure. I have arrested development, a youthful optimism that is challenged day after day—not without realization. I know what culture I am up against, and sometimes it thinks me to be a village idiot. A damn lucky one to be sure—a wife to subsidize his gross maladjustment, children who respect and love him, and yes, even a dumbed down culture that thrives in a super economy, where the daft painter can purchase expensive supplies on easy credit.

But geeze Louise, just stop for a day and assess the treadmill. The status house, the wealth lie. Lately I have been sitting on my life "Indian style", that is, with adult lifelong conviction that we are all living on the "Res" in one way or another. Supposedly, after shelter, food, clothing, fuel, and modern medicine, we are educated to free our minds, find our place, and flow helpfully in society. In my extended clan of the past or future I would fit in as one of the radical-clowns, one to see the black and white of the situation, re-act to it, voice it, color it in the proportion that I see fit, and send it over to the wise council for deliberation. However, this reservation is casino corrupt. It silences many good Indians with humiliation that is usually enough to set them on a path to unrighteousness, to unlove, to uncourage, to unjoy.

I am getting off track. I want to write about the writer and painter as radical-clown. But first, to clarify my position above... A distant Indian relative of mine said it best:

Not long since, a strolling Indian went to sell baskets at the house of a well-known lawyer in my neighborhood. "Do you wish to buy any baskets?" he asked. "No, we do not want any," was the reply. "What!" exclaimed the Indian as he went out the gate, "do you mean to starve us?" Having seen his industrious white neighbors so well off—that the lawyer had only to weave arguments, and, by some magic, wealth and standing followed—he had said to himself: I will go into business; I will weave baskets; it is a thing which I can do. Thinking that when he had made the baskets he would have done his part, and then it would be the white man's to buy them. He had not discovered that it was necessary for him to make it worth the other's while to buy them, or at least make him think that it was so, or to make something else which it would be worth his while to buy. I too had woven a kind of basket of a delicate texture, but I had not made it worth any one's while to buy them. Yet not the less, in my case, did I think it worth my while to weave them, and instead of studying how to make it worth men's while to buy my baskets, I studied rather how to avoid the necessity of selling them. The life which men praise and regard as successful is but one kind. Why should we exaggerate any one kind at the expense of the others?
—Thoreau

Exactly! Hence, the Indian in the country, weaving his baskets.

After a near-perfect anniversary celebration I had the usual rush of "fear in the financial future" that afflicts all of the unmade artists of the world. It is the downside of happy delusion, and I think a very needful sorrow for the creative mind to be up against. Without it, there can be no fight, and it is the fight that can bring you back to right-thinking. The next day I decided to bring some self-published books and lessor paintings out to sell along the land's impressive road frontage. Businessmen always ask about road frontage before buying. Very important consideration. It can make or break what seems to be a sound business plan. Anyway, the seasonal Renaissance Faire is a quarter mile up the road and brings an enormous amount of traffic past our country property on weekends in summer. We let our friend Dan sell his tie-dyes there, and he does quite well. Last year I joined him three times, about 25 hours of retail work, and made 40 dollars total. I sold one book and two paintings. (Actually, just the two paintings. I threw the book in for one customer because I was just so damn happy to sell a painting.) In comparison, Dan made about $400 during the same period.

I imagine the Ren Faire to be a good random sample of local Caucasian consumers. The bad history, horrendous detail, and several thousand turkey legs call out all strata of our class society—the college professor as well as the successful Quicky Lube technician. Dan gets about 2 customers per hour on average, with at least one purchase, maybe a t-shirt or a onesie. A hundred dollar day is nothing to sneeze at. So, the Indian businessmen would work with Dan's model, improving upon it, making a mint for the family and clan. The Indian radical-clown however, after failing with his business model, does it again for good measure.

And ho boy, does he succeed at repetitive failure!

Not one customer. 500 cars drove by, all headed to the same place, to spend money on the same stuff. SUV's and Audi's. F-150's and RV's a-plenty. 75% of the cars driving by cost about what we are asking for the land. Perhaps 75% of riders in the cars could name this year's American Idol winner, and 75% would ride off a cliff if the last bag of Cheetos® on earth was leading the way.

I had a memorable anniversary. I love Marie. We will keep the land, grow our debt, and live as free as we can in a super economy on the American reservation. I am the radical clown who makes joy in the head. I'd say "Pleased to meet you", if you ever got out of that pathetic rusting cage-on-wheels to interact with a radical clown.

Farewell, Ye False Deceitful Joys 2014. Acrylic on canvas 36 X 24"

Day Trip To See Winslow Homer Paint Rich People Problems

Spent a bright summer day with a friend touring the Burned
Over District from Cazenovia to Cooperstown. Beautiful country.
Rolling hills, green and lush, manicured farms, hops and sheep
herds. The land loved by four generations of Throops—I'd set up
housekeeping there too if I was a rich man, that is, one who could
make a living from the land, without the 100,000 dollar investment in the John Deere Corporation. We pretended to be accom-
plished, well-received painters and wore ascots while we dined at
the Otesaga resort hotel.

Deborah Goldsmith was a young portrait painter before mar-
rying my Great Great Great cousin George Throop in 1832. She
would visit local homes on Saturday and paint the likenesses of
Mr. and Mrs. Farmer. She wrote poetry and like a good neighbor, was deeply religious at a time when God was both a glorious
deathless day and smite-on-a-whim. She died very young, leaving
two children for a school teacher to raise. His mother "adopted"
the daughter and son, while George sought work as a teacher in
any town that would take him. He did this for several years finally
making a move to Chicago to find fortune among relatives (one, a
cousin and future founder of Cal Tech). He died of an unknown
sickness a couple years later, orphaning his kids to his mother and
her second husband.

The letters George and Deborah wrote back and forth during
courtship are so revealing and supportive of my hypothesis that
intellectual and expressive evolution of humanity hit an apex at
some point in the 19th century. George, the farmer's son, wrote his
first love letter in May, 1832, a twenty-one year old Throop on the
chase. Deborah wrote back often too. She, even more literary and
thoughtful after a one-room schoolhouse education. I have several
of their letters. I post George's declaration below, followed by my
first love letter to my present-day wife of fifteen years this week.
I had a modern liberal college education. George learned to read
and write and do arithmetic on a hard chair without plumbing or

electric light.

Miss Deborah Goldsmith
Toddsville, New York
(Paid 10 cents)

Hamilton
May 20th, 1832
At Home.

Deborah:
It is with sincere pleasurable feelings that I now seat myself to
scratch a few thoughts to an absent friend, one whose moral worth
is beyond the reach of the deceiving machinations of the fawning
sycophants, whose heart is averse to the flattering deceptions of a
coquette, whose mind is raised above the fogs of sense and grovel-
ing desires by the light of science; whose soul has been filled with
that Love which was manifested on Calvary's rugged mount for a
lost and ruined world, where was crucified a loving Savior, where
was spilt the precious blood of Jesus for sinful man.

This morning my mind is deeply affected with a melancholy
scene before me (which I will mention in postscript), and the
dreadful calamities that daily roll themselves through this community, today beholding a disconsolate widow mourning the
loss of a kind husband and dear friend, with two little orphans
hanging around her, while their father lies before them a corpse,
stiffened in the cold grasp of death, never more to smile on them
nor embrace them in the arms of affection. These things affect me,
and when I turn on the other hand and see a multitude engaged in
the pursuits of life, some after the gaudy bubble fashion, some, the
shining dust of earth, others trampling on slandered innocence, it
all tends to wean me from the deceptions of a flattering world and
to examine my own deceitful heart.

This is a beautiful morning in May. The earth is carpeted in
green. Everything is starting anew to life. All nature is clothed
in beauty. The forest, after braving the furious blasts of winter, is
now mantled in a beautiful green. The little foresters are skipping
from branch to branch with joy and gladness. They hail the morn

with songs of praise and bid the setting sun adieu with their sweet choral symphonies. The blossoms are unfolding their beauty to the morning sunbeams and everything is calculated to call forth the feelings and present to the mind of man the wisdom and goodness of our Heavenly Father. When I behold such harmony throughout creation, I am convinced, as even past experience has demonstrated, that 'tis friendship that sweetens the joys of life, sincere friendship, a principle of the heart. It smooths the rugged pathway of life, quells the stormy passions and opens in each heart a door from which all that is delightful, all that is pleasing, all that is consoling, all that is amiable, all that is virtuous, flow. For what? To be spent in air? Or to float down the broad stream that rolls itself to the briny ocean, and there to be buried in oblivion? I answer, No. It is, rather, to cheer the desponding heart of mortal man and convert him from a downcast misanthrope to a sympathizing friend, and thus bring him home to the enjoyment of society. Although there is a great deal said about friendship, it affords consolation to none but the virtuous, the sincere. To all others, the reverse.

That you may not mistake my meaning, I now declare unto you in the words, my sole object in engaging your company. It is to obtain a friend, a friend to share with me the joys and sorrows of life; to cheer in the hour of gloom and be glad in the hour of joy; to gain heart and hand, and travel with me down the declivity of life, and, when fortune frowns and I am buffeted about on the stormy ocean of adversity, one who can look with a smile and console the tempest-beaten bosom with cheering conversation.

Yes, Deborah, this is all that urges me forward, and will it surprise thee when I declare that in thee my desires center, and all my hopes of earthly happiness have an end? After mature consideration and closely examining my own heart, I find that thy friendship and thy presence will ever be delightful. To know that thou art willing to comply with this request and impart thy virtue in increasing the happiness of one who respects virtue's innocence, is all that will make life delightful to me. I claim no perfection; such as I am, I offer myself and thus make manifest my desire.

Deborah, I wish not to draw from thee a hasty and inconsiderate answer. No, take your time to consider. It is an important point; on it hangs all our future happiness. But this I claim: 'Tis truth I send, and truth I ask in return. Perhaps you may think I am asking too much, but please to inform me if I am on the right ground, or not. So I add no more.

Adieu.

Yours sincerely,

George A. Throop

P.S. — Friends in health. Write soon as convenient.

P.P.S. — Died, on the 19th inst., of the bilious fever, Mr. Hiram Niles, aged about 32. He left a wife and two little children. His sudden death is truly afflicting to the sorrowing friends, and to all rendered more so by the state of his mind. Lived about two miles south.

George (21 years old)

And finally Great Great Great cousin Ron, 163 years later, still a Throop on the chase:

August 10, 1995

Ms. Rose, Rosa es una Rosa es una Rosa,

By now it is no secret that I am drugged with the thought of you, and that I need sleep, a good long one, for your drug to wear off. Someone or something slipped you into my drink, and after an onslaught of embarrassing hallucinations, and my heart's suffering of those bittersweet palpitations, I feel the need to explain myself and the series of dreams I've had of you...

"How can I keep from singing?"

You are a strange one missy. I don't know you beyond my thoughts of you. Still, that cannot stop me from flashing these pictures of my madness. That is urge, and to me that is normal. I haven't the courage to ask you for a cup of water or a piece of pie, but I have the nerve to explode before your eyes, and that isn't fair, and life isn't fair. So I am rather crude because I reject the preliminaries of "getting to know someone". I know how to set myself up for a great fall.

Though before I carry on, and reveal to you the great big fool that is me, please, to save you the embarrassment, ignore my babble flat out. Just sit down someplace reflective with this paper in your hand and view it like you would a passing bird, a gray cloud, the noise of a car... Maybe think of this as a gift, like a painting of a squirrel suspended in mid-air. Or, put it in storage like an ugly lamp Aunt Tulip sent you for Christmas. Don't abandon it entirely though, at least not until you've tested its light.

"Shhh" is the command for this day. I haven't the least bit of feeling for myself. You cannot hurt my feelings.

Oh, by the way, if you were wondering...This is Ron, the cook. Listen to this...

"Sometimes with one I love, I fill myself with rage, for fear I effuse unreturn'd love;
But now I think there is no unreturn'd love—the pay is certain, one way   or another;
(I loved a person ardently, and my love was not returned;
Yet out of all that, I have written these songs.)"—Walt Whitman

I think that makes sense, right?

Well now, to announce my crush...

The other night on your stairs I got up and took a walk into your neighbor's yard. I left you a little something on their porch a while back. I thought it was *your* house and porch. I hope that whoever lives there has a good sense of humor. Obviously they haven't any tact.

There are so many ways to look at something, to sense it, drink it in, digest it. I am a quiet fellow on the outside, shy, absolutely inarticulate in every way, but in no way does that account for the inferno bubbling inside of me. Eyes tell all, which is nothing if you're not an eye-reader. And, as your eyes have it, I remind you of our distinguished first president. Fine. My teeth are strong, an off-yellow perhaps, and crooked like my character. To look at me from a distance, you would swear my torso rests on thin air. My legs are paper thin yet strong. They get me from here to there effectively. You know all about my hairs, or lack thereof, and I hope to God I have kept my nose clean. Personal hygiene and I haven't been very close friends these days. It is my curse to be more concerned with the waxing of the moon than with the wax build-up in my ears. I have a heart feeling the power of Aldebaran and arteries that push an Amazon or a Mississippi. This always gets me into trouble. "Heart of mine so malicious and full of guile; give you an inch and you take a mile..." I do my laundry when I run out of clothes to wear, and whenever I become infatuated by a woman's presence, I let her know right away. Or at least after a year of restless sleep and abnormal wanderings. I am a pile of contradiction, and I have nothing of any value to offer you. I am a fantastic liar. An even better loafer! I'm sure that on a date I would bore every mite off of you.

There you have it! An introduction to the self I am. Why is my desire so strong? Well Rose, you are human, like me, and I am sure you'll be very relieved to hear that I have not constructed any pedestals for you. You're a bit under a foot shorter than I, and I like it that way. However, I want you to know, even if you have been told a thousand times already, that you are *fine* and desire sucks... But only to the point when you begin to shoot in the dark at an idiot who is leaping in the dark. I am afraid of separating you even further away from me than you are now. Ouch! That would be bad. I like your talk. Your heart is big. Enough said.

Except for this: Please understand... There is no way you can let me down. So don't even try you beautiful fool. I am not asking for anything you have not already given, splendidly. This letter then? Well, this is just a gift to you. Take it as it is. Hell, I'm not even asking you out on a date! That should bring you some relief, eh?

Look, I am a poet and I sing. I can hope that you can hear. Cheers.

Ron (27 years old)

James Mott Via PTSD Mutilates Young Henry's Politics 2014.
Acrylic on canvas 36 X 24"

Vanity 2007. Acrylic on paper 17 X 12"

Humanity Vanity

Last night my wife and I watched the movie *The Wolf of Wall Street*. There is no review forthcoming. Just a statement to heal me this morning. Already very late after the three hour frat party of a film ended, I tossed and turned in bed for an hour thinking up ways to inflame and insult Martin Scorsese, the dirty old man of Hollywood who gets paid a mint to make soft porn movies because he is rich and powerful among other near-death dandys of the same race and gender. They, like Scorsese, are honored among themselves in late life for being humanities' media crime bosses. I imagined Martin appearing in my house, strapped to a chair, while I danced by him every ignorance and stupidity of American culture I could think up, taking short breaks to shame him the best I could. How good of him to leave us this niche hell of a movie so late in life. How proud his pre-pubescent great grandchildren would be discerning reality between Santa Claus and glorious pretend quaalude sex with hookers. I would ask him man to man how it feels to be in a room directing other millionaires and thousandaires to gang bang like hallucinating monkeys. Is his tongue loll obvious? Is his casting couch still in operation, or do even the most desperate starving actresses cringe at the thought of his wrinkly old man body?

If I want *The Wolf of Wall Street* in real life I just need to think back to the middle stall in the bathroom of my college Alma mater. There I could find the writing, the plot, the degenerate stories told by that class of Americans who get rich to get old to die unfulfilled, alone, pathetic and sometimes even disgusting. And the Academy will make sure a special tribute is offered. Multiple millions of the world's comfortable proletariat will be taught by a few loud dogs of humanity what constitutes culture for their remaining quiet nights at home before blowing out a final breath. If I died in bed last night, my Crazy Horse moment would include the memory of a lit candle stuck between Leonardo DiCaprio's butt cheeks, or the CGI erection of his pudgy supporting actor who pretended to masturbate in front of a film crew at the behest of the great and powerful Martin Scorsese.

Confusion. Enough reality confusion each day while children are bombed by cowardly governments and I sit beside grown men who espouse the virtues of a Walmart Supercenter. And for entertainment digestif, a multimillion dollar three hour movie depicting a rich man's vile madness—either a wolf of Wall Street or a Martin Scorsese. I could always turn it off, but it would not shame the losers of society any more or less. All peoples connected to that movie, from pipe fitter to enthroned producer, must answer to their own progeny somehow, someday. Martin's inner circle, the troop of Leonardo aficionados, even the beer buddy of Rick the stage hand will, in life, insulate their leader like all the President's men. And it will make a good life if the R(reality)-Value is laid on thick enough. Hollywood wins, in life. However, Scorsese has already marked his posthumous legacy with a deep and heavy familial shame. He's flipped off every child of his line born innocent with the added boast, "I helped make this world you come into. As an elder, with my fame and riches, I normalized insanity. This is what I think of you Great Grandchild. Enjoy Hell. At least I had a great time".

Loathsome dregs of society like Martin Scorsese bypass our judgment while they carry a loud vanity into old age because each and every one of us is a Martin Scorsese.

I'll give Henry Miller the last word. From his preface to Parker Tyler's 1944 book *Hollywood Hallucination*:

"We credit the Hollywood nabobs with being Machiavellian, because they pander so successfully to the low taste of the mob. We pretend that there is an unholy partnership between Church, State, Factory and Cinema, and the pretension is just. But get a close-up of these cruel, cunning arbiters of our destiny and you get a picture of Everyman when he has emerged from his larval state. They are all walking the treadmill, all harried and ridden, all responding with automatic inflexibility. You have to feel just as sorry for the Pope, or a toothless Rockefeller, as you do for the Georgia convict or Bertha the poor sewing machine girl. The Hollywood stars and the men who promote them toss in their sleep with the same unremitting anguish as the street-walker and her pimp. And while Hitler is at large we all do the goose-step with good grace— all except Mahatma Ghandi who, according to the zombie logic, must obviously be out of his mind."

Yeah, I agree. We're all nuts. I can still hope Scorsese's grandchildren shun his memory tomorrow for the living dog he is today.

If I Were Mao, I'd Make Lawyers Eat Tainted Bananas To Put Bad Rash On Face 2014. Acrylic on canvas 18 X 24"

If I Was Mao, Art Ruby Would Post My Work For Its Playful Style And I Own An Army 2014. Acrylic on canvas 18 X 24"

**Dear Members of the Hiring Committee, and Ms. Clarion,
Or, Why I Don't Get Hired Ever**

I am writing to apply for the position of Assistant Gallery Director. As a graduate of SUNY Oswego, a half-lifetime resident, as well as a professional painter and writer, I believe I am a strong candidate for consideration. I know the area very well, and reside on Sheldon Ave, adjoining the boundary of campus.

From recent study and reflection about Tyler's future, I feel that my efforts via guidance of the present director and art faculty could dress up the gallery to significantly improve its image as regional player in the visual arts.

I am a painter and writer, who has exhibited regularly over the past six years and published several books. I have been the sole promoter for many of my shows, and have personally prepared and installed exhibits.

Whitman wrote condemning our reluctance to self-promotion:

"...Under the broadcloth and gloves, under the ribbons and artificial flowers,
Keeping fair with the customs, speaking not a syllable of itself,
Speaking of any thing else but never of itself."

He went door-to-door peddling *Leaves of Grass*. I feel that people are inherently reluctant to sell themselves. Still, I have kept at it like a trooper, learning what there is to know about self-promotion, mainly, that I don't like it one bit. However, I have quite the opposite feeling when asked to promote the work of others. Finally to forget about me, me, me and sing the praises of those most deserving! I admire so much about art and the artist, and am able to give glowing reviews to any who are brave enough to enter into a career of creativity. I feel that lightly goaded I could go out into the street to excite people about what Tyler has to offer this season. I come to the shows once in a while. There I encounter the usual suspects. The regulars. Fine and good, but the gallery needs to expand its efforts to become better recognized. Community outreach would be at the top of my plan. On campus I would focus on a cross disciplinary approach. Every work of art and the artist herself has a history that can be attributed to the teachings of more than one or two departments in a liberal arts curriculum. For instance, I came to Tyler for a show of artist Kara Walker's work back in 2009. It was well attended even though she couldn't make it and sent a grad assistant to speak in her stead. She is an artist of international fame. I wonder how many English, History, Psychology, Sociology and Economics professors and students attended. I feel that the college missed out on a wonderful opportunity. And the community? Again, just the usual suspects. And yet upstate New York and Oswego in particular have a strong connection to slavery's past. The ghosts of Frederick Douglas and Harriet Tubman are an evening's drive away. Gerrit Smith built a library across the river on the condition that it not exclude anyone by race or gender. Certainly prejudice, sexism, and racism have not gone away. Work by Ms. Walker was an opportunity for several department professors to engage their students, using the past to comment on the present and predict future trends. Yet the gallery was not even half full for an exhibition that should have opened up Waterman, and hired a sound and light crew for her talk.

Art is powerful when people are active with it. I would introduce myself to professors across the campus, and let them know I am there to assist in any curriculum wherever I believe art crosses its path.

The community has several school districts with teachers who would benefit by introducing their students to the gallery's programs. I would form relationships with art teachers across several counties.

Another anecdote. Last fall, Mike Flanagan invited me to a talk by Elizabeth Smith-Boivin, Executive Director of the Northeastern Chapter of the Alzheimer's Association. He asked me to invite any others who would be interested. I sent out personal e-mails to every health care facility in Oswego County and several in Syracuse, also nursing homes and assisted living complexes alike. I included an invitation and an attachment of the promotional flyer. I did not receive one reply, nor witness any attendance to the lecture akin to my effort. Her talk was very informative and would be a boon to any who work in elder care facilities, psychology fields, the pre-med sciences, and even business majors here at the college who seek careers promoting mankind rather than the bottom line. I mention this to point out the weakness of the Internet in event promotion. The web is a bulletin board for updating the verve of your venue. Nobody waits with bated breath for an institutional invitation from cyberspace.

For all talks and exhibitions sponsored by Tyler, I would personally seek out those who would benefit from it. Print media and Internet mailings aside, nothing beats a handshake and a face-to-face exchange. Still, I am quite good at the former as well.

I am confident in my ability to promote Tyler visually across the Internet as pertains to social networks. Presently its Facebook page could use a face lift. The first comment visible rates the gallery page very low, and to add insult, is written by a local photographer and high school art teacher. Likewise, the last official post was made in October. Not a very good first look at the gallery from a would-be attendant, nor prospective artist for that matter.

I could not locate a Tyler Art Gallery Twitter link. As Assistant Director I would tweet from the gallery every working day, like Thoreau, to "...brag as lustily as chanticleer in the morning" about the programs at Tyler.

That is to say, I would be very active online promoting the college galleries. I have had some professional success at Twitter and Tumbler. Roseanne Barr has favorited my work, and The MoMA has put two of my images on their Tumbler page. Not bad. Roseanne and one of the greatest art houses in the world.

I enjoy the wide breadth of personality that make up a living, active art culture. Hosting artists visiting Oswego would be a pleasure. I would be enthusiastic when organizing field trips to other galleries and museums, engaging with students on the art exhibition committee, and making myself approachable not just to Studio Art majors and Museum Studies minors, but to all students on campus. Art is for everyone, not just for those seeking a way of life within it.

I would be a hard-working assistant to the gallery director, performing all duties required of me cheerfully and with determination. My best quality is enthusiasm. My second best is a sense of humor. I can connect on many levels with faculty, administration, and a college student body. While moonlighting as a professional artist myself, I would bring informed perspective to those just starting out on an art career.

I am eager to find out more about the position of Assistant Gallery Director. I look forward to an interview. No doubt my hands will be sweaty. Once over that hump, however, I am sure to leave a favorable impression.

Sincerely,

Ron Throop

Candidate For State Senate Joe Dyer and My Burgeoning Insanity

Joe Dyer is running for State Senate * in the 37th district of New York State. My friend Pat called me up yesterday to say so. He read Joe's biography while I sat in a brown chair, my mind spinning into overdrive, contacting memory, learning, and philosophy to process the new, personally pertinent information. Joe was our peer all through elementary and high school. He was a dandy, and a mean one at that. I believe the word "preppie" came into use during eighth grade. A preppie would be likened to a "soc" from the book *The Outsiders*, still assigned reading for kids today, as if there are no contemporary teen fiction authors worth their salt, and its author S.E. Hinton is some kind of generation leaping teen guru of eternal wisdom.

Though tall and long-armed, Joe was no physical in-your-face bully. But he was mean. Disdainful. Stuck-up was the term to designate elitist young people back then. Joe was an effeminate young boy, which confused many of the other kids, but at that tender age, not enough to turn their confusion into cruelty. Our families all had more or less an equal amount of disposable income, so other, more finesse, status lines were drawn. The preppie click started young, fourth grade in my school. It was all due mainly to geography and dress. Joe hung around with the girls of the same development. There was money in these houses, not a great deal more than the rest of town, but enough to improve upon the kid's wardrobes. Joe and his girl friends had the latest from Izod*, Levi's*, and the ever-cool sounding OshKosh B'gosh*. They sported a high fashion that all the kids coveted but most were unable to acquire by the fifth grade.

Salvatore was a friend of mine, who had recently moved into a big house in Joe's development. For a stretch of several months I went over to his house most days after school. We practiced disco in Sal's living room and walked around the development pretending to be fifth grade cool. Often Joe would be out with his gaggle of well-dressed girls taunting Sal with the mean kid slang of the time like, "Why are you hangin' out with gay-boy Throop? He's a fag—Tell him to go home." To Sal's credit, he always defended me.

Sal didn't think I was gay. Neither did I. Who knew what homo-sexual was anyway? I may not have been gay, but I was definitely a romantic. In school I sent Lisa, one of Joe's girl friends, a carnation on Valentine's Day. She wasn't ready to be loved, at least not by me, and so defensively called me a gayboy in reaction to the flower gift, which was unfortunate because of her position as trend-setter at our elementary school. Joe, Lisa, and the girl friends shared their prejudice to other preppie boys and girls, and together they fash-ioned quite a scary hell out of my elementary school experience.

Joe Dyer remained a condescending peer throughout the rest of our hometown school years. As I recall, by graduation, be-yond being an impeccable dresser, he never stood out in any way but average. According to his biography he went to Georgetown University for his bachelor's degree, and received a Master's in International Affairs from Columbia University.

Here is some Joe Dyer professional life story straight from his Senate® campaign Facebook®:

As Senior Vice President of Global Policy for Visa, Inc.®, Joe launched the strategy to open the China market for American financial companies, which became a landmark case at the World Trade Organization (WTO)® that the U.S. won. For over a decade at AIG®, he served as a Director of Corporate and International Affairs where he worked hard to open foreign markets to U.S. goods and services. This helped create good jobs back in America.

Joe was then appointed to serve as a Senior Advisor and Chief of Staff to the Under-Secretary for Domestic Finance in the U.S. Department of Treasury® from 2003 to 2005. He returned to AIG® in 2007 and planned to spend the rest of his career there focused on expanding business in international markets. But, like many regu-lar employees, he lost his job during the financial crisis and was left with only his personal integrity, resolve and entrepreneurial spirit to provide for his family in the highest taxed county in the nation. He learned how losing nearly everything can sometimes provide you with even more, if one is willing to work hard and pursue the American Dream.

And finally, the reason why Joe is running for office, accord-ing to the little lying satan perched on his left shoulder:

Joe Dyer is running for New York State Senate * to bring the voice of regular, hard-working families back to Westchester. He knows what it means to balance a budget, hold the line on spending and create jobs by opening new markets for American products.

A veritable saint of a man, Joe Dyer.

That should be enough about Joe for me to leave his memory the heck alone. But I am feeling a bit feral today. Wild in many ways not akin to Joe, but in the sense of unbelievable why and mega-stupendous how. How can Americans be so politically and philosophically drained of even a drop of reactionary dignity? Why is Joe, the stuck-up nothing special preppie of my memory poised to have influential power in state politics as well as the wealth and status of Croesus? The people of Joe's über taxed county have a choice between two candidates to represent them this November, and one of them was high up in a company that took nearly a tenth of a trillion dollars of tax payer money in a bailout. A couple weeks later the candidate may have been spotted at The St. Regis Resort in Monarch Beach, California enjoying a half a million dollar spa vacation with other jolly, upbeat executives. And if he wasn't there in person, in spirit he was more responsible than anyone else in his district for the financial crisis of 2008.

So many darting reactions to Joe's social success. I need to take hold of one and fly with it.

In my artistic, fatherly, husbandly, morally, joyfully non-humble opinion, I believe Joe Dyer to be the scourge of the earth, the antithesis of good, a representative of King Beelzebub if anyone anywhere still actually believed in the domain of Hell. Joe is my spiritual enemy because to a sensitive painter and poor man he can be nothing else. What he sees as accomplishment, I have spent a lifetime countering, for I sincerely believe that his achievements stand up as the earth's only evil. Joe Dyer is avarice incarnate. In my little world of control, the means always justify the ends; one reaps what one sows, etc. Privately, Joe will get his just desserts someday, but in the mean time—Oh, in the mean time!

I am working on an exhibition of my paintings protesting the probable arrival of the natural gas industry to upstate New York. I am not getting paid. My wife and I are investing in all the materi-

als and time necessary to express my deep concern for the future
of our water supply. Joe Dyer, if insanely elected, and if ready to
tow his parties' line, could be the deciding vote to lift the present
moratorium and clear a path to the monster nature-haters. This
fracking hoard will make their millions, while laundering a piece
of profit back to Joe and his cronies, under the guise of improving
the economy for simpleton Jack the corn farmer. And then when
the fissures crack, and all the gas has risen, and the pools have
brought childhood leukemia to the gay boys and girls of his grandchildren's childhood, Joe Dyer will have been long since dead,
laid to rest some time ago with the rich man's understanding that
there is no retributive justice for the people ever. Joe Dyer must
envy me much more than I want his money. He knows he makes
nothing but trickle-down sorrow for so many people of the earth.
He must know too, privately, that his money and power is not self-
made. For Joe Dyer it was all luck, placement, and yes, hard work,
but toward nothing, nothing, nothing of eternal merit. There are
only so many hours in a week, and for Joe Dyer to resumé such a
life means he neglected all the life wonders that I hold dear to my
heart. If he is as good a father as I, a better husband, a gentler soul,
then let the earth ram its pin-hole into the sun, for I must be a
crazed lunatic.

Americans suffer from a live and let live psychosis. It must
be evolutionary, from a time way back when we had to subsist in
small clans for survival, and we trusted, intuitively, all characters of the tribe. If Joe Dyer was to gain business respect in 8,000
B.C.E., he would have to be one of the best wampum stringers, for
he certainly could not come of age as a warrior or wise man. And,
since wealth was shared by all, the chief would have ordered his
banishment the moment Joe wove his first Izod® alligator mocca-
sins. Individual status was achieved with reason and consent of the
tribe, not acquired through billion dollar bureaucratic contracts or
their equivalent, which at that time of course, did not exist.

That constituents of the 37th district of New York will even
step out of their cars to vote for Joe Dyer, and not blow up the poll-
ing station for the fascist insult made to their children and their
children's children by the initial placement of Joe, is how I can tell
that this crackpot civilization is finally kaput.

When executives of British Petroleum®, via Halliburton® negligence, kill eleven people on an oil rig, while choking the life of the gulf of Mexico and beyond for millennia to come, and yet not one Joe Dyer dandy among them spends an overnight in a Mississippi county jail cell, then the race has finally achieved an evolutionary reverse-jump. It is on a moral leap back to monkeydom.

Just a couple years before that tragedy, powerful friends helped their monetary equals at AIG* to the American till for 85 billion dollars, a sum that distributed responsibly could do a positive good for the nation, perhaps end homelessness or supply age care to all grandparents in need. Yet no storming of the Bastille ensued. Not a peep from the masses. Not one justice stoning of any Joe Dyer involved.

Today my moral adversary runs for state office on the Republican* ticket claiming the desire to represent hard working Westchester County families, even after public knowledge that his darling institutions are directly responsible for the high taxes they pay. It is such a tall irony that it has broke my mind into the realm of the silly-absurd.

Joe Dyer is not a good man. He is a bad man. Not because he is rich but because he is rich. He is a liar. He does not wish to represent working families. He wants to enslave working families on his international financial plantation of woe because it means a purchase of a yacht for him. I hate Joe Dyer and despise his society because it has become a topsy-turvy world of anti-justice for the many, and manipulation of all wealth and power toward the central class. You are all gay boys and girls to Joe Dyer. You are below him. He believes success is directly proportional to wealth acquisition. Fortunately, this belief can only evolve into a parasite infecting the entire culture if we believe it too.

Unfortunately, a broad majority do.

Yes, like Jimmy Cliff, even the poor poet-painter wants his share of what's his. But he will never get it, and justly so, if he thinks good of what Joe Dyer's got. After over twenty years privately observing the human comedy, Ron Throop has come to the conclusion that great wealth can only come to the average, the predictable, the steady and of course, the corrupt. Joe represents a new species classified by Linnaean Taxonomy, and will pass on its characteristics to his unlucky progeny. Let me see if I can get this right. Joe is progenitor to *homo smiling scumbagus*, an up and coming species of Armageddon.

Dear Joe Dyer, contemporary public figure of my condemned youth, I wish you continued success on your neo-con psychopath of the über-rich. My only regret in this memory of you is that I did not split your lip when we were small.

The painting below I re-purposed upon hearing the news about another bad apple rotting to the core.

The Joe Dillon Improves Society Like Beelzebub Nurtures Puppies! 2014. Acrylic on hard board 24 X 32""

Central Park Stroll Arm In Arm After Fine Meal At Restaurant Daniel 2014.
Acrylic on canvas 18 X 24"

Central Park Stroll Arm In Arm After Fine Meal At Restaurant Daniel And Hyperallergic Is Not Much About Art

Hyperallergic hosts a Tumblr site which claims it will post some of the art made by its loyal followers (the peopns) every Tuesday. The human creatives beyond Brooklyn or Manahatta that "do" art out of reach of the wafting pee stink. Artists of everywhere else on earth who go for walks to be inspired or because they are inspired, and can duck into the woods if the bladder demands it. Poor New York. Not one free public toilet outside the library. It is failing people and art, and it knows it. New York Art has made itself a visual "hit" on a smart phone, and most of the people hitting it are the uncreative "entertain me, I'm bored" twenty or thirty somethings in excellent dental health. Foolishly I have clung to its crumbling art world/market paradigm for several years, but am forming new opinions. For me the definition of New York art today could include the phrase, "the desperation of phony". Its own "world's greatest New York art blogazine", as Hyperallergic deems itself, spent the entire day Tuesday posting mostly crap, almost as if to prove that there is no creativity anywhere but in New York. There was a fast sketch self-portrait of a man who repurposed a piece of loose-leaf garbage, and to his astounding clever credit, drew it while blind. There was a photo taken of what looked like a jogger's legs upside down in a park garbage can. Also, an article about a katydid in Ancient Greece, and a cartoon to suggest that throwing away your smart phone will improve creativity. Other stuff too. Articles and info pertaining to nothing really. Maybe inspiring a "wow," or a "woo," or a "neat" from the hoard of uncreative click-ers roaming the streets. All day it published a total of five images by actual followers, of which the site boasts of having nearly 48 thousand.

Fine if I haven't been uploading new images every Tuesday for six months. Also fine if the blind self-portrait on the piece of garbage was comparable to the hundreds sent in by those artists praying to get "made" by the best New York art blogazine in the whole wide world. However, there was one post yesterday that proved to me Hyperallergic's irrelevance among all things art and artists alike. That it is a gossip column, or a Bill O'Reilly culture war team member, I have no doubt. At its best, it could work well as a New York Times "outsider" affiliate, the anti-establishment establishment for the establishment. The Whitney could love it for both its museum worship and seasonal Christie's love story. And I would leave Hyperallergic well enough alone to exist under those auspices. I even forgave it once for posting a street art painting of Batman and Robin kissing. For sure, we all want a better world, and who is to say that the dynamic duo drawn as gay men is not art? At least it was a drawing, a painting, a sculpture, or any medium at all that the world would know to be art. But one post yesterday is not art. Not even close.

It was a video GIF of Ray Rice, the football star, running in place. Below was written the Hyperallergic editor's take on domestic violence. Not that any of us asked for it. We post on Tumblr so we can share our work to a wider audience. Many of us are able to leave the studio most times without unholy urges to beat up on our wives and husbands. We go to Hyperallergic hoping to get a big break into the New York art scene. Instead we get Ray Rice the non-artist. The million dollar football man. The wife-beater. Could Hyperallergic at least attempt the search for David Hockney video whacking the shins of his partner with a galvanized pipe? Aren't there any wife-beating artists we can read about? None at all? Probably not. The editors of Hyperallergic follow some culture blog, like the N.Y. Times, and repost the celebrity gossip because it's easy. But it is not art, nor representative of art in any way whatsoever.

Dear Mr. and Ms. Editor of Hyperallergic, sane men and women do not like to beat each other up. Retarded football players might face punch their wives, sure, but they're not making art about it. When I was young I witnessed an off-duty cop acquaintance cold cock his wife onto the muddy ground at a Grateful Dead concert. My girlfriend and I had just arrived in California. The acquaintance took us up to San Francisco and paid for the concert tickets. How were we to know he was a wife beater? And geez louise, he was a cop, not an artist. But that is the only time in my life that I had to witness domestic violence beyond what my wife and I do to each other when we're really, really mad. Thanks for the video. Got it. Not art. Just another reminder that domestic violence has not gone away.

On that same post, scrolling down a bit, the following is written over the unart video of Ray Rice running:

"Romantic Love Was Invented To Manipulate Women"

Hence the Central Park painting above, my partner and I strolling arm in arm—my *romantic* partner and I—dreaming the evening away after a perfect day and an early dinner at a famous restaurant that we saved up for all year long. I never imagined that I was manipulating the girl I dreamed about. I must be a bad man.

I suck the painter's sour grapes every day. In fact, I think I could be addicted to rejection. But look here Mr. and Ms. New York elitist pretend artist editors, don't you ever, ever mock the painter's devotion to romantic love. It is what has made me non-existential. It is what brings me depth where you lack in taste and true culture.

Terry's Funk Shirt I Wore For 2 Years While I Am Bipolar
2014. Acrylic on canvas, 16 X 20"

Painting Show Friday Night a lá Stuckism

Opening up the house again for painting's sake. I hope the art and writing students at the college on the hill stop by. They should see what they're up against. In the past five years I have spent a few thousand dollars in promotion alone to encourage my peers to come out of their shells. The over-insulated shells with high r-value—32 avarice, 21 professional jealousy. Every show I send out invitations to professors at the art and English departments, pin posters up all over town and college, post the event in newspapers and radio, prepare foods, decorate, sing—a veritable hyper-clown of delusional preparation. Always the same outcome—several good friends, family, and one or two brave hopefuls. I am lucky to have anyone come by. Lucky and daft.

The past two mornings I have been painting fast "studies" on discarded press-cleaning sheets. I have ten and will charge $10 a piece. This will pay for the wine and cheese.

Look here, art and artist can become a philosophical act. Last week a stuckist peer on the other side of the country referenced a quote of Picasso's: "I would like to live like a pauper with lots of money". I have been living that thought my whole adult life. All artists do, but not all those who "make art". Riches could be substituted with the word's "clan approval", if we still lived clan-like without nomadic faux-status acquisition; if we were still local to the land, and needing real human support.

I guess that is my purpose with painting and hosting these shows whenever the urge strikes. The artist as fool attempting to connect his neighbors in joy. To become dependent on each other for comradeship.

If any of you have read the book *The Joy of Man's Desiring* by Jean Giono, then you know that I am pining for a world like Grémone Plateau. Yes, I am Bobi, but a little bit of Jourdan too.

Or, like Inger in *Growth of the Soil* by Knut Hamsun, we need to live to find our niche without Dunkin' Donuts fueling our blues.

All stuckists at heart invited! Country wines uncorked and pouring.

KI + 2S —> KISS 2014. Acrylic on canvas 36 X 24"

Dan And Sally Welcome The Intellectual Season To Cole Hill 2014. Acrylic on canvas 36 X 24"

KI + 2S —> KISS

This September and October I have been painting my Great Grandfathers of Madison County, N.Y. This title pertains to Henry Grosvenor Throop writing words of wonder into his journal on February 3, 1900. Four generations of my father's family lived in Hamilton and surrounding villages—it was a great place to be in the 19th century. So many triumphs of the future began in Central New York. I am making a painting for each grandfather who lived and died there.

In this painting Henry is dreaming of the night before when Mr. Hatch loaded thirteen boys and girls onto a bobsleigh, hitched a team of horses and took them on a midnight ride to Hamilton. He left several of the boys (Henry included) at Colgate Academy to continue their studies into the spring. Henry wrote of the night:

"We had Will's big team and a bobsleigh with a big box and plenty of blankets. I had the darndest time I have ever had and so did some of the other people. [A line of his secret code I have not yet deciphered]. We were packed in like sardines in a box. There were 13 in the lead. It snowed and we had to raise umbrellas and do other things to protect us from the storm [more secret code]."

On the next page he writes:

"The following reaction is said to take place by the union of potassium iodide and sulphur, under slight pressure:

KI + 2S —> KISS

This is a dangerous experiment and should not be tried in direct sunlight or where too many people are near."

Henry was twenty years old when he wrote this. Proof that a hundred years ago there was innocence past teenhood. I have a theory about cultural evolution, which the study of local history will corroborate. Our culture has gone into degeneration hyper drive. Each generation past Henry's has exponentially surpassed the one before it in debauchery. We are in fast decline. It is the teens I wish to impress with these four paintings of my ancestors. Delve into their own past to discover a world their parents forgot. The simple made extraordinary, the everyday sublime, knowing that cholera or consumption could take the most robust life on a whim. Yet even in isolated Hamilton of the digital age it seems nigh impossible for our young to keep the Nicki Minaj machine from encroaching deep cleavage upon their best dreams.

Colgate University could do a good turn for future generations by killing its Wi-Fi connection and reinstating practical subjects like agronomy and electrical engineering into its liberal arts curriculum.

Fat chance. Even university president John or Jane worship the iPhone like a god.

If I Was Mao, December 25 Would Come Twice A Year. We'd Ransack The
Houses of Millionaires And Call The Day "Mao-mass" 2014.
Acrylic on canvas 24 X 18"

Yes Minik, I Will Avoid The MoMA Like Tuberculosis 2014.
Acrylic on canvas 36 X 24"

Yes Minik, I Will Avoid The MoMA Like Tuberculosis

In 1897, the Inuit boy Minik came south to New York with his
Dad and four friends at the behest of Robert Peary, the north pole
fibber. Within a few months, all but Minik died from colds gone
pneumonic and T.B.'d. The Museum of Natural History delivered the bones of Minik's father, Qisuk, upstate to Cobleskill to
be bleached in a fast running stream. It (the institution) staged a
mock burial of Qisuk for Minik's sake, while gluing Qisuk's bones
back together for a public display about the Eskimo.

Several years later when Minik found out that his father was
loitering permanently at the museum, he petitioned its director
to give the bones of Qisuk back to him. He wanted to perform a
proper burial for his Dad. The director refused. The institution
refused. So Qisuk stayed in New York, his dead parts stolen by
people who always pretend to be good, but they just have a lot of
money and power.

Minik died from Spanish Flu in 1918. It wasn't until 1993 that
the bones of four Polar Eskimos were returned to northern Green-
land.

Painters beware. The MoMA is just a mere 2 miles away from
people who would claim ownership of someone's dead father, even
in an age of planes, antibiotics, and spaceships. Don't give them
yourselves no matter what the temptation. The administrators
there are hungry in a bad way just like their counterparts up the
road.

Beware. Especially during Halloween. Hold on tightly to your
bones.

Gourd Vase Wants You To Buy A Paper Painting 2014. Acrylic on hard board, 11 X 14"